To—
KRYSTAL AND CORY AND FAMILY
from CHLOE GEE.

P9-ECP-437

MacGregor's Book
Nook Discard
202 North Main Street
Yreka, CA 96097
(530) 841-2664

Happiness Is
a Family Time Together

LOVE YOU!

Happiness Is a Family Time Together

Lois Bock and Miji Working

Illustrations by Ron Riddick

Fleming H. Revell Company
Old Tappan, New Jersey

Scripture quotations identified KJV are from the King James Version of the Bible.

Scripture quotations identified RSV are from the Revised Standard Version of the Bible, copyrighted 1946, 1952, © 1971 and 1973.

Scripture quotations identified LB are from The Living Bible, Copyright © 1971 by Tyndale House Publishers, Wheaton, Illinois 60187. All rights reserved.

Words from "Something Beautiful," © Copyright 1971, by William J. Gaither. Used by permission.

Words from "I Love Trash"—Words and music by Jeffrey Moss. © 1970 Festival Attractions, Inc. Used by permission.

Excerpt from "Three Days to See," by Helen Keller is reprinted by permission of The Atlantic Monthly Company. The article was published in the January 1933 issue of *The Atlantic Monthly*.

The excerpt from *Making Religion Real* by Dr. Nels F. S. Ferré is used by permission of Harper & Row, Publishers, Inc.

PEANUTS cartoon is used by permission of United Feature Syndicate.

Library of Congress Cataloging in Publication Data

Bock, Lois.
    Happiness is a family time together.

    1. Family—Religious life. I. Working, Miji, joint author. II. Title.
BV4526.2.B58   249   75-22059
ISBN 0-8007-0761-3

Copyright © 1975 by Fleming H. Revell Company
All Rights Reserved
Printed in the United States of America

TO

Fred, Stephen, and Jonathan;
Ken, Randy, Russell, Jay, and Jeffrey:
For encouraging us to become
all that God has intended us to be.

Contents

Preface   9
Tips for Parents   11

1 Getting Started   13

Unit 1   I'M AN IMPORTANT PERSON

2 Important Because I'm Unique   19
3 Important Because I'm Talented   25
4 Important Because I'm a Friend   30
5 Important Because I'm Made in God's Image   34

Unit 2   OUR FAMILY IS SPECIAL

6 Special Because of Who We Are   41
7 Special Because We Have Fun Together   46
8 Special Because We Can Share Our Feelings   50
9 Special Because We Hear and Care   55

Unit 3   LIVING THINGS GROW

10 We Were All Small   61
11 Keeping the Windmills of Our Minds Oiled   68
12 Good News and Bad News   74
13 Faith Is a Living Thing   82

Unit 4   AT HOME IN THE WORLD

14 God Made It for Us   93
15 He Left It in Our Hands   97
16 *In* But Not *Of*   104
17 Ambassadors of God   111

Unit 5   BEING IN GOD'S FAMILY IS SPECIAL

18 Special Because We Are Adopted   119
19 Special Because We Are Freed From Guilt   123
20 Special Because God Lives in Us   127
21 Special Because We Are Christ's Body   132

Unit 6   WE HAVE A FUTURE

22 Not So Far Away   139
23 Understanding Your Story   144
24 Treasures Are for Finding   148
25 God Has a Plan   152

26 Evaluation—What Have We Learned?   157

Preface

Uncle Max recently delighted us by sending a journal of his years as a "printer's devil" (apprentice) on my father's newspapers in the Dakotas and Montana Territory. This gave us many insights into what both were like as young men, but it also reminded me of all the questions I never asked Daddy before he died in 1962. Why did he make the decisions he did? How did he *feel* about things? How did God come to be such an important Person in his life?

In *Happiness Is a Family Time Together* Lois and I want to give families an environment in which to discover God and each other in a relational, experiential way. Dr. Paul Jewett, professor of systematic theology at Fuller Theological Seminary, says that "revelation is God self-disclosing." We hope that the exercises in this book will help us to self-disclose, to come out of hiding—in the warmth and safety of our own families. We see this as a unique opportunity to know what the others around us *think* and *feel* as well as what they *do*.

We believe that in order for families to be successful in a growth experiment such as this, they must share the goals, and so (as in contractual learning) we include a "contract" or covenant as a starting point. (*See* page 16.)

We're also committed to the idea that *hearing* something is only the beginning of learning. We attempt to give opportunities for one to discover the concepts in each lesson, to reinforce them by verbalizing them, and, as often as possible, to act them out in some way. What a family can experience or model for a limited period can be extended to all of life.

MIJI WORKING

Tips for Parents

In calling the family together for these sessions we are calling them from other things that vie for their attention. We hope that they will respond because they find these sessions fun and rewarding. Most children (whether they are able to say it or not) would rather have your time and attention than anything else—including television.

Making this a good experience will require that the parents spend time in preparation for each session. Most of the materials are things that you will find in your home. Several of the sessions mention personal scrapbooks for each child in the family. This scrapbook can either be a simple construction-paper folder with several sheets of paper tied in with yarn, or one that you purchase. Keep these with your *Happiness Is . . .* so that they will be handy when needed.

Occasionally, special treats or outings are suggested, so it is helpful to read over the session a day or two ahead, especially the WHAT WE WILL NEED section. Everyone will enjoy it more if he has a special part, so you might want to note in the margin the roles assigned to certain individuals. Of course, you will always want to give each a part in which he or she can succeed. For instance, nonreaders will enjoy getting the materials together or being in charge of passing them out.

Try to surround the whole experience with fun. Challenge one another to a game of checkers while you're waiting for everyone to assemble. Or put on a record that everyone will enjoy. Give your family the freedom to laugh and joke during these times. It isn't necessary to be solemn to learn a spiritual concept. And a dark mood is not what you want to make this a positive and valued time.

Always try to state a question more than one way. First, read it as it appears in the lesson and then rephrase it. For instance: "What are some good characteristics of friendship?" could be rephrased as: "What do you think makes a good friend?"

While *you* don't want to habitually answer every question first (you may say the very thing someone else had in mind), if there is an unusually long period of silence, you might say, "Let me try this one. . . ."

If you find that certain family members are answering most of the questions, you might preface an inquiry with something like, "Let's hear from someone who hasn't answered yet," or "Johnny, you try this next question."

Probably the most important thing is to establish an atmosphere of trust. Don't use what you learn during these times of intimacy against one another. That is, as a cause for ridicule or punishment, or even the innocent use of quoting to others "the cute thing Kathy said about God the other night." As trust grows, so will freedom. ". . . where the Spirit of the Lord is, there is freedom" (2 Corinthians 3:17 RSV).

These times are for *shared* self-revelation and growth. No one person should be a target for either evangelism or behavior changes. These times will provide the opportunity, and the Holy Spirit will provide the work. Hopefully, the entire family, together and individually, will grow towards that wholeness called maturity. May this be a wonderful and exciting adventure for your family. Ask the Lord for this. He won't let you down!

1 Getting Started

Where We Are Going

Every session begins with a definition of the purpose or the goals for the time. In this initial session, these are the goals:

- To evaluate the time that you are now spending together as a family.
- To decide what the purpose is for your weekly family sessions.
- To give everyone in the family an opportunity to commit himself or herself to making these sessions successful.

What We Will Need

- Paper for each person
- Pencils

Note: This section should be checked by the leader before these sessions begin each week.

FAMILY SHARING

Give each person a blank piece of paper and a pencil and ask him or her to complete the following sentences. (Young children can give their answers verbally after the others have written their answers.)

1. If I have something important to talk over, I . . . .
2. I have questions about God and faith, but . . . .
3. Sometimes I don't say how I feel about things because . . . .
4. If I could change one thing about my family . . . .

When all have finished, take one question at a time; go around the room sharing your answers. This is a good time to remind the family that there is no *right* or *wrong* answer—just each person's honest reaction. Arguing, correcting, or ridiculing anyone's contribution can't help but hamper communication. The same is true of such comments as: "You *shouldn't* feel that way," or "You *ought* to. . . ." With acceptance and encouragement given to everyone, an atmosphere of trust and openness will grow.

Pastor Harley Swiggum, founder and director of Adult Christian Education Institute, which has brought the intensive Bethel Bible Study courses to hundreds of churches, startled us with a statement recently: "One hour in the living room with the parent talking about Christian concepts is worth six years in Sunday school in terms of effectiveness." That's how valuable an influence he feels the family is in molding a person's spiritual outlook.

Ken and I know this well, and yet I have to confess that we haven't had a very good track record in getting the boys together for a daily family devotional time. With four teenagers, our evenings are riddled with the usual church, Scout, and school activities. Ken's ministry includes many breakfast meetings, so mornings are out, too. We also have memories of our early years as Christians when we read *at* the children. Often the boredom or frustration of sitting still for these daily "lectures" defeated the very things we were seeking—closer family communication and a deeper spiritual life.

This year we began to notice that some of our richest spiritual times together were when we were learning from one another in a casual family dialogue—perhaps discussing a difficult passage of Scripture or maybe just how each of us felt about something going on in our lives or in the world around us.

We also found that while *daily* sessions were almost impossible to schedule, it *was* realistic to set aside an hour together once a week.

How about your family? When would be a good time for you to meet? Talk about these things after you answer the following questions. (Go around the family circle and share after asking each question.)

1. What do *you* hope to get out of these times together as a family? (Or, what would you like to see happen?)
2. What would you *personally* have to do to make that happen?
3. Are you willing to do it?

If you have all agreed to do this by meeting faithfully, you are making a *covenant* with one another. That is, a promise to each other and to God to be open to one another and available to one another. Does this seem risky—especially when we think of including God in the covenant? But listen to these encouraging words:

. . ."Cheer up, don't be afraid. For the Lord your God has arrived to live among you. He is a mighty Savior. He will give you victory. He will rejoice over you in great gladness; he will love you and not accuse you." Is that a joyous choir I hear? No, it is the Lord himself exulting over you in happy song. . . .

Zephaniah 3:16–18 LB

Perhaps you will want to list some things now that will help to make these family sessions successful.

HOW TO MAKE OUR FAMILY TIMES WORK

1.

2.

3.

4.

5.

6.

7.

8.

Family Growth Covenant

We the _____ family, covenant to meet regularly for the purpose of knowing one another and the will of God better. Unless unusual circumstances prevent, we will meet each _____ day, at _____ o'clock. The signatures below show our willingness to take part and make this time a helpful one for our family.

Signed:

SEAL OF APPROVAL

Unit 1

I'M AN IMPORTANT PERSON

2 Important Because I'm Unique

3 Important Because I'm Talented

4 Important Because I'm a Friend

5 Important Because I'm Made
   in God's Image

2 Important Because I'm Unique

Where We Are Going

Many people live each day with a feeling of defeat and inferiority, because they have never been made aware of their own uniqueness and value. We sincerely feel that God intended for us to know of His love for us and of our personal importance. This cannot start too early in one's life. It is our desire that you take time to establish in your own life and the lives of your family members the foundation of self-confidence and faith in your Creator and the uniqueness and value of His Creation.

What We Will Need

- Pencils for each person
- Paper for each person
- A box of crayons or colored pencils
- Colored construction paper
- Yarn or string

FAMILY SHARING

Begin the session by having someone read aloud these words of Jesus:

> Not one sparrow (What do they cost? Two for a penny?) can fall to the ground without your Father knowing it. And the very hairs of your head are all numbered. So don't worry! You are more valuable to him than many sparrows.

Matthew 10:29–31 LB

Anyone can answer the following questions:

1. How do you think God feels about birds and other things in nature?
2. Jesus says, "*You* are more valuable. . . ." Without getting into what the Bible says in other verses, why do you think God would value people more than birds? What makes people better?

Now have someone read this passage:

> Long ago, even before he made the world, God chose us to be his very own, through what Christ would do for us; he decided then to make us holy in his eyes, without a single fault—we who stand before him covered with his love. His unchanging plan has always been to adopt us into his own family by sending Jesus Christ to die for us. And he did this because he wanted to! . . . . Moreover, because of what Christ has done we have become gifts to God that he delights in. . . .

> Ephesians 1:4, 5, 11 LB

3. List the ways we can know from this passage that we are important to God. (Explain the word *adopt* if there are small children in your family.)

4. This selection tells us that *we* are presents to God, and that He is happy with this gift from Jesus. Can you think of things you like about each one in the family that God would like, too? Have one person at a time sit in the middle of the family circle, as the others in turn tell what each likes about him or her. Have the Family Secretary record this on the following page entitled: WHAT MY FAMILY LIKES ABOUT ME.

WHAT MY FAMILY LIKES ABOUT ME

Names	Comments

We have a vivacious, charming Director of Education at our church. A few weeks ago a little boy walked into her office. She greeted him by saying:

"Hello, my name is Peggy Cantwell, what's your name?"

"Brian!"

"Well, I'm so glad to know you, Brian."

"Why?"

"Because God made you a unique person. There's only one you, and I would hate to go through life and never know the only you."

When God created you, I wonder just what type of pattern He used. One thing I do know—He never used that pattern again. You are an original and there are no copies made of you.

Have someone read aloud:

> You made all the delicate, inner parts of my body, and knit them together in my mother's womb. Thank you for making me so wonderfully complex! It is amazing to think about. Your workmanship is marvelous—and how well I know it. You were there while I was being formed in utter seclusion! You saw me before I was born and scheduled each day of my life before I began to breathe. Every day was recorded in your Book. How precious it is, Lord, to realize that you are thinking about me constantly! I can't even count how many times a day your thoughts turn towards me. And when I waken in the morning, you are still thinking of me!
>
> Psalms 139:13–18 LB

5. How does that paragraph from the Psalms make you feel?
6. Why do you think that God chose to make different individuals, when He could have made us all look, think, and act alike?
7. Divide the family into twos (unless there are only three in your family—then put three people to a group) and ask each other the following:

   - The best part of my day is. . . .
   - The one thing I look forward to the most is. . . .
   - My personality is unique because. . . .
   - My looks are my very own and I am different from you because I have. . . .
   - I like to think and learn about. . . .
   - My relationships to my family and friends are important to me because. . . .

Now "introduce" the one you interviewed by telling the family how he or she answered each question.

FAMILY FUN

Have someone read aloud:

When I was a teenager I had the privilege of meeting Dr. Henrietta Mears, College Department Director for First Presbyterian Church of Hollywood. Even though she was well into her seventies at the time, she was the most vital, exciting person I had ever met. One day I asked her how she made friends so easily. Her reply will always stay with me. She said with her usual enthusiasm, "Whenever I meet someone, I imagine that I see a sign tied around his or her neck. The sign says: MY NAME IS———PLEASE MAKE ME FEEL IMPORTANT."

She had a great idea! Now let's each make a sign with our name on it and hang it around our necks or pin it to our clothes.

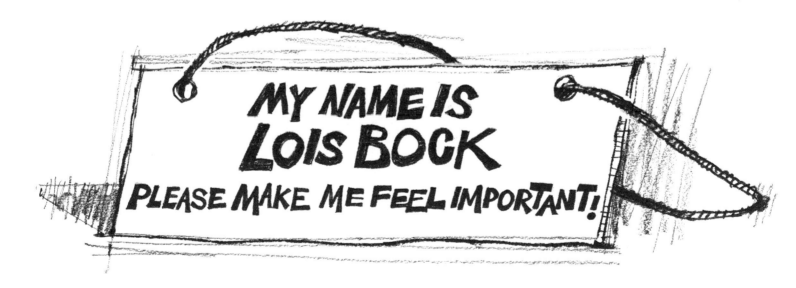

Do you know that you are a very special person? While you work on your signs, can you think of some reasons why you are important? Think of at least one characteristic or thing about yourself that you like. (It might be one mentioned earlier by someone else.) You might show this on your sign by drawing a picture, and share this important characteristic with your family.

24 HAPPINESS IS A FAMILY TIME TOGETHER

Together Before God

With eyes closed and heads bowed, thank God in a word or phrase for the things you are grateful for in His Creation. After several minutes, when all have had a chance to thank God for something, the leader can close with *Amen*.

ASSIGNMENT

During this coming week, imagine each person wearing his or her sign. If you should feel that people are forgetting to appreciate each other, get out your sign and wear it so that your family can be reminded to try even harder to make each other feel important.

3 Important Because I'm Talented

Where We Are Going

Our goal and purpose is for each of you to realize that you have talent, what your talents are, and to recognize the talents of others. We also want you to understand the responsibility that accompanies talent.

What We Will Need

- The leader should fill in the sign-up sheet for the talent show and post it in a convenient spot. Place a pencil or pen with it.

FAMILY SHARING

This would be a bleak world without talent. Our lives are made more exciting, easier, and worthwhile because we can create and we can use the talents of other people. I just looked around the room where I am working (which happens to be our den), and I can see many results of talent. There is a wall lined with books because writers have put their thoughts down on paper for our benefit. There is a lovely, framed poem about the birth of our son, Jonathan, which our neighbor, Chris Neff, wrote and gave to us. Also hanging on the wall is a very special song which has been written for our family by our friend, Mary Caldwell; and Midge Mebane's bright, cheerful oil painting does wonders for a bare, off-white wall. Our cabinets are full of records and tapes—many of these were done because of my husband Fred's talent. And in the next room, reading a six-year-old-type story to our son Stephen, is another person with talent—Louise Hill has a unique way with children; she makes living fun for them.

Look around you right now. Each person to share your feelings about the talent in your surroundings. As a family answer these questions:

1. What do you see in your home that is a result of talent?
2. Who is responsible for the creative contributions?

Have someone read the following aloud:

Again, the Kingdom of Heaven can be illustrated by the story of a man going into another country, who called together his servants and loaned them money to invest for him while he was gone.

He gave $5,000 to one, $2,000 to another, and $1,000 to the last—dividing it in proportion to their abilities—and then left on his trip. The man who received the $5,000 began immediately to buy and sell with it and soon earned another $5,000. The man with $2,000 went right to work, too, and earned another $2,000. But the man who received the $1,000 dug a hole in the ground and hid the money for safekeeping.

After a long time their master returned from his trip and called them to him to account for his money. The man to whom he had entrusted the $5,000 brought him $10,000. His master praised him for good work. "You have been faithful in handling this small amount," he told him, "so now I will give you many more responsibilities. Begin the joyous tasks I have assigned to you."

Next came the man who had received the $2,000, with the report, "Sir, you gave me $2,000 to use, and I have doubled it." "Good work," his master said. "You are a good and faithful servant. You have been faithful over this small amount, so now I will give you much more."

Then the man with the $1,000 came and said, "Sir, I knew you were a hard man, and I was afraid you would rob me of what I earned, so I hid your money in the earth and here it is!" But his master replied, "Wicked man! Lazy slave! Since you knew I would demand your profit, you should at least have put my money into the bank so I could have some interest. Take the money from this man and give it to the man with the $10,000. For the man who uses well what he is given shall be given more, and he shall have abundance. But from the man who is unfaithful, even what little responsibility he has shall be taken from him."

Matthew 25:14–29 LB

3. Think about this story that Jesus told. Please express what you think He was trying to tell us.
4. Go around the group and share what you feel you have been given as special talents.
5. How are you being responsible and using your talents?

Have someone read:

And if, as my representatives, you give even a cup of cold water to a little child, you will surely be rewarded.

Matthew 10:42 LB

Again, Jesus says that we should be faithful in giving what we can. A person who gives just a cup of cold water to a little child is giving of a talent—to serve others.

6. What one person has given to you of his or her talent? What did he or she give, how did they give it and how were you benefited? Write your responses here.

7. During the coming week, how can you give of your talent to another person? Write your goals here.

FAMILY FUN

This portion of our lesson will have to come later. Plan a FAMILY TALENT SHOW. Decide when and where right now. Each person select one thing that you can do best and prepare for your part in the show.

Here are some suggestions: Can you ——
    give a reading?
    write a poem?
    paint a picture?
    write or sing a song?
    plan and prepare a delicious dessert?
    show a prize plant or animal?
    fix something that is broken?
    really clean a room?
    make a new dress, tie, or pillow?
    do a collage using old magazine pictures?
    tell a funny story or joke?
    play a musical instrument?
    arrange a bowl of flowers?

Whatever your talent is, present it to your family. And—your family promises to be a very good audience. Here's your chance to be "onstage."

Have someone in the family make a poster telling the time and date of your FAMILY TALENT SHOW and pin it up as a reminder. Are there any special friends you would like to invite?

Additional note to the leader: You may have to help someone in your family discover what he or she can do—especially a young child. It is important that no one feels inferior or left out of the group activity.

4 Important Because I'm a Friend

Where We Are Going

Each one should realize because of this session that: He or she invests in people when he makes a friendship; he has responsibilities to his friends; his friends affect his view of himself.

What We Will Need

- Pencils
- Whatever supplies each may need for FAMILY FUN

FAMILY SHARING

When the Working family visited Death Valley last Easter vacation, we, like thousands of other tourists, were fascinated with "Scotty's Castle." This stone mansion, complete with tower and moat, is filled with art treasures and valuable furniture from Europe. Part of our fascination was at finding such an estate in this barren isolated spot. But more than that we were intrigued by the story of the unusual friendship it symbolized.

Scotty was a prospector who apparently never found gold, but found something even more precious in his friendship with William Johnson, a millionaire who came to Death Valley for his health. Johnson was asked once if Scotty had ever paid him back the thousands of dollars he'd loaned him to grubstake (or finance) his many ill-fated ventures. "Yes," Johnson replied, "with thousands of laughs."

Each of us has friends whom we *grubstake* by investing our time and interest. Go around the room and answer each of these questions, taking one question at a time, allowing about five minutes each for questions 2 through 4:

1. Who are your two best friends outside of the family?
2. Why do you like having them as your friends? What do they contribute to your life?
3. Why do you think they like having you as a friend?
4. Is each of these friendships a fair exchange, or does one person have to give more than the other to be a part of it?

Death Valley Scotty made a list of rules for himself that he felt made a good friend:

- Never say anything that could hurt another person.
- Never give advice.
- Never complain and never explain.

Jesus had many things to say about what makes a good friend, too. Here are some of them: (Leader might have someone else read these aloud.)

> Don't criticize, and then you won't be criticized. For others will treat you as you treat them. And why worry about a speck in the eye of a brother when you have a board in your own? Should you say, "Friend, let me help you get that speck out of your eye," when you can't even see because of the board in your own? Hypocrite! First get rid of the board. Then you can see to help your brother.
>
> Matthew 7:1–5 LB

> . . . . If you call your friend an idiot, you are in danger of being brought before the court. And if you curse him, you are in danger of the fires of hell.
>
> Matthew 5:22 LB

The greatest love is shown when a person lays down his life for friends.

John 15:13 LB

There is a saying, "Love your friends and hate your enemies." But I say: Love your enemies. Pray for those who persecute you! In that way you will be acting as true sons of your Father in heaven. For he gives his sunlight to both the evil and the good, and sends rain on the just and on the unjust too. If you love only those who love you, what good is that? Even scoundrels do that much. If you are friendly only to your friends, how are you different from anyone else? . . .

Matthew 5:43–47 LB

Now think of one-word answers to the question, "What do we need to be a good friend?" Have one of your good letterers write them at random below:

NEEDED FOR FRIENDSHIP

Taking the words from the NEEDED FOR FRIENDSHIP space, or others that you may think of, have each one in the family give a "gift" of one of these qualities of friendship to a member of the family. Then he or she should decide which one he wants to "keep" and tell why. Repeat until all have chosen a gift.

For instance, Mother may be offered *kindness,* *patience* and *acceptance* for her friendships. She might choose *acceptance* because she is aware of being a little critical of a certain friend.

Together Before God

After each has selected his "gift," have a time of either spoken or silent prayer as each asks God to help him to be a good friend to the people he named at the beginning of this session.

FAMILY FUN

Each person choose to do something nice for at least one of the *best friends* mentioned. This can be a thank-you-for-being-my-friend gift (any little thing), a card that you have made or have especially selected because it says "just the right thing," or baking cookies for the person. Anything you like— this week do something special for your special friend.

5 Important Because I'm Made in God's Image

Where We Are Going

To examine the following:

- The various physical forms God uses when He appears to man
- His mental facility as much as we can understand
- His emotional capacity
- His actions
- To understand in what ways we are like Him

What We Will Need

- Bible with slips of paper marking the verses you will read in FAMILY SHARING
- Pencils
- Sheets of paper

FAMILY SHARING

Our Stephen is an active, never-stop-thinking six-year-old. A few weeks ago he dribbled a basketball into the kitchen and said, "Mom, when you think of God, do you think of Him as a number or as a person?"

"Well," said his very busy mother (me), "I guess I'd have to say that I think of Him as a person because He made us to be like Him, so He must be something like a person."

"Well, I don't—I think of Him as an apple," Stephen stated with all the authority of a kindergarten graduate.

"An apple?" said his surprised mother.

"Yes! You know an apple has skin on the outside, and then the fleshy part that you eat on the inside, then it has a core inside of that—You see, it

34

has three parts and is only one apple. That's just like God—three in one!" And out he dribbled to his backyard court.

I'm sure that you don't have "apple theology" in your house, but how do you see God?

1. Give each person a piece of paper and pencil. Now take a few minutes to either write your personal description of God or draw a picture. When this is completed, share your thoughts with the rest of the family.
2. Have someone read Genesis 1:26, 27 from the King James or Revised Standard Version. Then have someone read the same passage from the Living Bible. What does the word *image* mean? Write your answer here.

3. God has actually appeared as a physical Being many times to some people in the Bible. Let's take a look at what form He takes:

To Abraham He was	(Genesis 17:1; 18:2–33)
To Moses He appeared as	(Exodus 3:2)
To Moses, Aaron, and Israelite elders	(Exodus 24:9–11)
To Moses and Joshua	(Deuteronomy 31:14,15)
To Gideon	(Judges 6:11–24)
To Isaiah	(Isaiah 6:1–7)
To Ezekiel	(Ezekiel 1:26–28)
Other physical characteristics	(Psalms 94:8, 9)

4. God has emotions, too. What are they?

Psalms 79:5
Proverbs 21:3
Isaiah 63:5
Hebrews 3:10

5. God can also think and reason. What can you find out about the way that God thinks?

Psalms 139:3
Psalms 147:5
Isaiah 1:18
Isaiah 29:15, 16

6. God is a God of action. What has He done in the past and what does He do today?

Psalms 19:1; Colossians 1:16
Psalms 35:10
Psalms 94:10, 11
Psalms 139:1–4
Proverbs 3:12
Nehemiah 9:17
Jeremiah 17:10
John 3:16
Hebrews 6:18

Please feel free to add any other verses to this study.

7. Since we are made in His image, each of us has something like God in us. Share with each other what traits you have noticed in the other family members. Write down your observations here:

8. You have all heard the expression: "He is the spit and image of his father." In the spiritual sense we call it *Godlike* or *Godliness*. What person most lives a Godlike life to you? Go around the circle and let each person tell his answer and what it is about that person that reminds him of God.

Personal Discovery

Each person take a piece of paper to be put back into a personal notebook. If you feel like sharing this section, you may do so, but it is basically for your own self. (*Parents:* For very small children, you will, of course, have to help them with this section and write down their answers.)

1. How am I personally like God?
2. How can I grow to be more like Him?
3. What can I do today?

FAMILY FUN

The most outstanding characteristic that we can discover about God is His love for us and His kindness toward us. Since we are made in His image, our FAMILY FUN section is to show kindness.

Your leader will write the following items on small pieces of paper and put them in a bag or a bowl for each person to draw. Take turns drawing a piece of paper, read yours aloud and then make plans to do whatever your paper says. (*Note:* If the leader can think of specific things or people to be kind to, please make up your own instructions.)

- Do a domestic chore that will make living in your house nicer for those who live with you.
- Visit a person who is lonely or ill and would enjoy your company.
- Write a letter to a person you admire and thank him for his life and the example he is living.
- Cut out a beautiful picture from a magazine, glue it to a piece of construction paper and give it to someone you love or put it in a place for the family to enjoy.
- Find a meaningful poem or prayer and give it to someone who could use some encouragement.
- Treat someone to an ice-cream cone or cookies.
- Take a flower to a neighbor with a note that says, "Thank you for being you."

Unit 2

OUR FAMILY IS SPECIAL

6 Special Because of Who We Are

7 Special Because We Have Fun
   Together

8 Special Because We Can Share
   Our Feelings

9 Special Because We Hear
   and Care

6 Special Because of Who We Are

Where We Are Going

Each person should know something of his background and of the family traditions that have been built. We also feel that each person should know of the personal history of his or her parents, how they met and why they chose to establish a family unit.

What We Will Need

- Bible
- Paper for individual scrapbooks
- A copy of the Family Tree (can be made ahead or each can make his own)
- Pencils, pens, or marking pencils
- Paper
- Special family recipe and whatever ingredients are needed for the family cooking
- Map or globe

FAMILY SHARING

As a family answer the following questions:

1. What is a family? Write your definitions here:

2. Have someone read the following:

Then the Lord God caused the man to fall into a deep sleep, and took one of his ribs and closed up the place from which he had removed it, and made the rib into a woman, and brought her to the man. "This is it!" Adam exclaimed. "She is part of my own bone and flesh! Her name is 'woman' because she was taken out of a man." This explains why a man leaves his father and mother and is joined to his wife in such a way that the two become one person.

Genesis 2:21–24 LB

Who do you think invented the idea for us to live as families?

3. Why do you think God thought this was a good idea? What benefits do we have when we belong to a family?

The creation of your family is a link in the chain of God's overall Creation. On the following page is a shortened version of the chain of God's Creation. Starting with the Adam-and-Eve link, fill in the others with historical figures and end up with your own family. Think of this not as a precise genealogy, but as a family-of-man chain.

4. How did your own family begin? This could be called the Family History Class. And it is Mom and Dad's turn to answer the questions (with someone else reading them, if possible). So parents (and other adults in the family circle): Please answer the following questions:

   - Where were you born?
   - What was your family like?
   - What did you like the most about your family?
   - How and when did you meet each other?
   - Where did you have your first date?
   - What one thing about the other person first attracted you?
   - How did you know you were in love?
   - What were the details of your wedding?
   - How did you feel when you were married—happy, frightened, excited, and so on?
   - What goals did you have for your marriage?

5. Each person brings to a marriage a different background, a different set of traditions and culture. What types of background were brought into your family? Is there German, Italian, Mexican, or other descent in

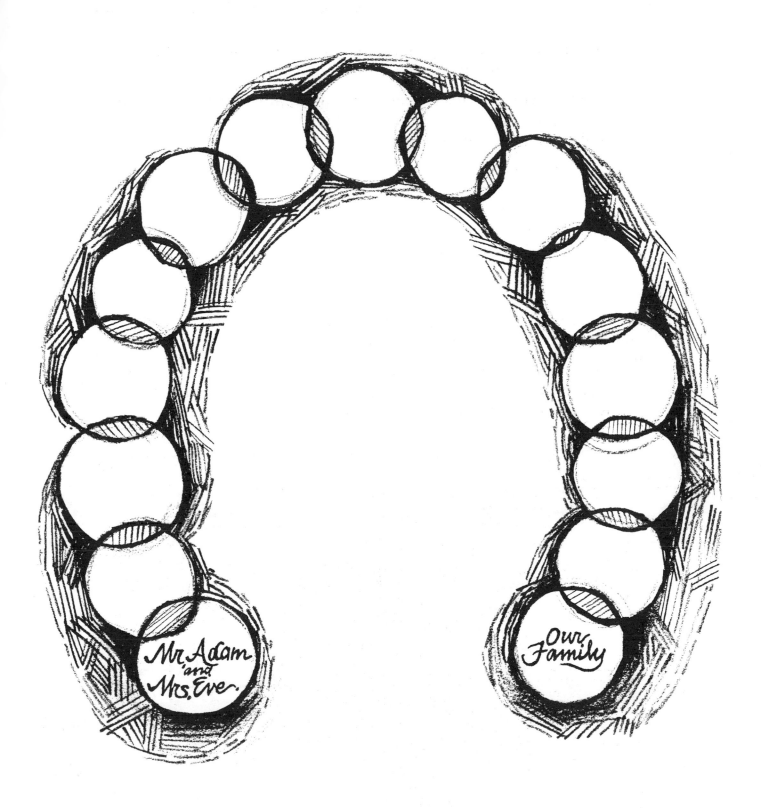

your family? Talk about this and if necessary point out the various countries represented on a map or globe.

- What nationalities or countries are represented in the family background?
- What are the special traditions:

  Religion?
  Food?
  Stories?
  Songs?
  Occupations?

FAMILY FUN

Each person will receive a paper for his notebook or scrapbook. The page should be entitled: MY FAMILY IS SPECIAL

1. There is a Family Tree for you to fill in or to copy. That's the first thing to put in the book. Your parents will help you with that now. Remember the trunk of the tree is for your name.

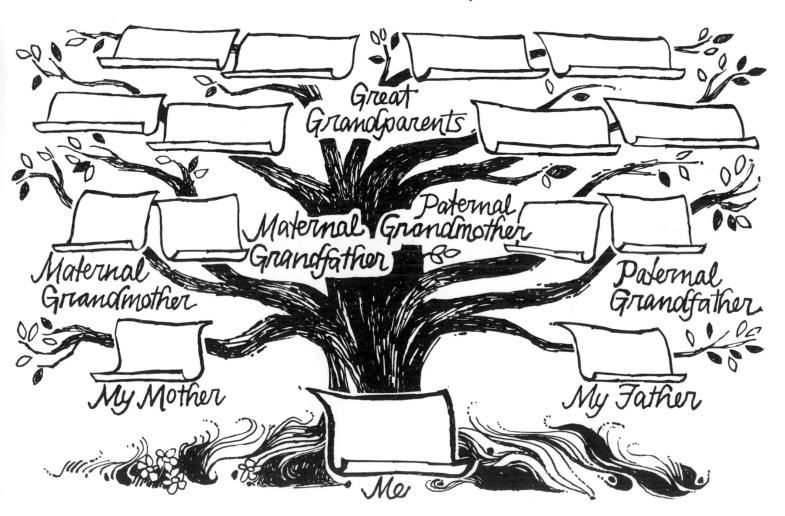

2. If the children of your family are old enough, have each one write a paragraph about the family and put it in his or her scrapbook. Tell the number of people, the names, and what you most like to do together as a family.

3. Draw a picture of your family and describe the drawings to each other. (*Note to parents:* This is a good time for you to see how your children view the family. Is one person more outstanding than the others; does one look especially gloomy to the artist? Observe but don't comment.)

4. What is a dessert that could be called a family favorite? Now we want you as a family to go to the kitchen and whip up this special treat. If this is part of the tradition of your own family, Mothers, why don't you make copies (or dictate) this recipe for the children to have in their scrapbooks and keep for a time when they can pass this on to their own families?

Together Before God

Join hands and thank our heavenly Father for our earthly family—for those in the past as well as those in the present. Pray silently or aloud, with the leader closing at an appropriate time with *Amen.*

██

7 Special Because We Have Fun Together

██

Where We Are Going

We want to learn to enjoy each other's company, to learn to laugh together and to learn to be creative in fun and pleasure.

What We Will Need

This will require some organization, but you will have to come up with your own list, depending on what you as a family decide to do together. Read FAMILY FUN for some ideas.

FAMILY SHARING

As a family, read the following quotations and answer the questions together:

1. What does the word *fun* mean to you? Write your *fun* definitions here:

The dictionary says that fun is: mirthful sport or diversion, merry amusement; joking; playfulness.

46

2. Did you know that the Bible says something about being merry? Have someone read the following:

A merry heart doeth good like a medicine. . . .

Proverbs 17:22 KJV

Talk about why being cheerful and merry has a good effect on us.

3. A professor by the name of Nels F. S. Ferré has said something very meaningful about family play in *Making Religion Real*. Have someone read this:

Happy are the families that learn to play. The family needs to play together. In play people are brought to one attention and to one level. There can be indoor games and outdoor sports according to age and circumstance: hikes, picnics, bicycle trips, all kinds of travel. There can be informal conversation, listening to programs together, going to worthwhile movies, plays, or musical entertainments; for smaller children, imaginative games unlimited. The son who now beats me at chess still remembers the fascinating boat races we had with twigs on the Neponset River when he was three. Playing together, whether it be actual games or reading together for fun or going to entertainment together, gives real cohesiveness to family life. Anyone too busy for such play is too busy to be married. Too busy to live, one cannot hope to find or make religion real.

FAMILY FUN

Now take a few minutes to plan something to do *just for fun*.

We Bocks are a family of four—two adults and two little boys. And we really do enjoy outings and special evenings. Sometimes we plan rather elaborate things to do together and then other times we just stay home and plan a whole evening of things to do together. Recently we got up very early one morning and took a train to San Diego to visit the animals at the zoo and Sea World. It was a great time.

We regularly plan special evenings at home like the one mentioned in point 4 below. We have a special dinner in the dining room with flowers and candles. I get out our best dishes and silver and we "dine" rather than eat together. It is a great time to learn about conversation and manners. After dinner, Stephen and Jonathan both select a game they would like to play. Stephen, who is our oldest, usually will choose a game like *Chinese checkers* or *Concentration* and then little Jonathan will almost always ask us to play *firehouse* with him. We sit on the floor in his room and build firehouses with blocks and logs and fill them with every fire truck in the house. We each take a make-believe name and role and we are off to the make-believe fires. After the games, we put away all the toys and we read stories to them until bedtime. These evenings are as much fun for Mommie and Daddy as they are for Stephen and Jonathan.

Here are some suggestions that will help you to come up with your own ideas. Be sure that whatever you decide, it is something that will include the whole family in the fun.

1. **Picnic to some lovely spot:**   Add to your family fun by preparing the food together. For one picnic that we had, I took gift boxes (about the size that a dress would fit in) and as a surprise decorated the boxes for each family member. This can be simple or elaborate. Maybe each person could decorate a surprise box for another family member. Or if your idea of fun for a picnic is just putting some food in a brown paper bag, then do that, but just have fun!

2. **A game night:**   This will vary with the ages of your children. We really have fun doing jigsaw puzzles and playing checkers. In the winter, we put a big plastic tablecloth on the living-room floor, light a fire in the fireplace, and have a "picnic" in front of the fire and play games together.

3. **Hikes:** If you live near an area that would be good for this, wear comfortable shoes and go hiking.

4. **A treat-the-family-like-company night:** Fix a super dinner, use candles, flowers or some appropriate centerpiece, and your best dishes. Maybe you could even do this with a theme from a foreign country—Italy, for example. Fix spaghetti, decorate the table with a red-and-white-checked tablecloth. (Use a paper one, if you don't have a cloth one.) Play Italian music during dinner if you have such a record or tape, and maybe you could have a discussion on Italy or Italian customs. If you have small children, point out Italy on a map or globe.

5. **A special play, concert, or circus:** If it is within your budget, maybe you could get tickets for such performances.

An important suggestion is to take into consideration *every* member of the family. Let each express what he considers to be fun and would like to plan.

Make a family announcement of the chosen activity and post it somewhere for everyone to see. ***Then just relax and enjoy yourselves!***

■■

8 Special Because We Can Share Our Feelings

■■

Where We Are Going

We want to see that all of our emotions are part of us and that sharing real feelings with those close to us brings us closer to each other and to Jesus.

What We Will Need

You might find this session more comfortable around the kitchen table.

- Poster board (about 20" by 32") or side of cardboard box
- Old magazines and glue
- Crayons or felt-tipped pens
- Scissors
- Construction paper, scraps, yarn
- Large grocery bags

FAMILY SHARING

Sometimes people think that in order to be a good person you have to smile all the time. It *is* good to smile, if that is the real way you are feeling, but what if you are really angry or sad? Then a smile is really a mask like the one you put on at Halloween. It hides your real face from those around you. To understand this, try these games as the Working family recently did:

1. Without explaining or talking about what each other says, finish these sentences in as many ways as you can think of in about three minutes each. (Don't take turns, just speak up as you think of things. This is called "brainstorming.")
   Joy is . . .
   Sadness is . . .

2. As you go on with the rest of the session, the family can be cutting magazine pictures that show these feelings—to be pasted on a board

50

divided diagonally. The top section can be lettered: JOY IS . . . and the bottom: SADNESS IS . . . .

3. Using large grocery bags, cut out eye-and-mouth holes. Decorate with construction paper or crayons, felt-tipped pens, or yarn. While you make your masks, think of the ways someone might put on an invisible "mask" so those around won't know what he is feeling.

4. Name all the ways you have felt in the last week and put them in the spaces below:

"GOOD" FEELINGS	"NOT-SO-GOOD" FEELINGS

"Oh, sure! " I heard my four teenage boys laughing mockingly in front of the television one evening and paused to see what they were making fun of. It was a replay of a show from a family series. One of the children in it had lied and caused a lot of misery for one of the others. When, at the end of the program, he was found out, the father calmly explained that this was a wrong thing to do. The wrongdoer calmly accepted this, and the sister he had hurt calmly forgave him as the mother looked calmly on.

My boys laughed, not only because they found this calm, emotionless handling of a tense family situation unbelievable, but also most unsatisfying. Real people have real feelings and *need* to share them with those closest to them.

Now read these parts of the Bible and write the feelings or emotions you think each talks about:

Then it was time for the annual Jewish Passover celebration, and Jesus went to Jerusalem. In the Temple area he saw merchants selling cattle, sheep, and doves for sacrifices, and money changers behind their counters. Jesus made a whip from some ropes and chased them all out, and drove out the sheep and oxen, scattering the money changers' coins over the floor and turning over their tables! Then, going over to the men selling doves, he told them, "Get these things out of here. Don't turn my Father's House into a market!"

John 2:13–16 LB

Feelings _____

When Mary arrived where Jesus was, she fell down at his feet, saying, "Sir, if you had been here, my brother would still be alive."

When Jesus saw her weeping and the Jewish leaders wailing with her, he was moved with indignation and deeply troubled. "Where is he buried?" he asked them.

They told him, "Come and see." Tears came to Jesus' eyes.

"They were close friends," the Jewish leaders said. "See how much he loved him."

But some said, "This fellow healed a blind man—why couldn't he keep Lazarus from dying?" And again Jesus was moved with deep anger. . . .

John 11:32–38 LB

Feelings _____

Then Jesus brought them to a garden grove, Gethsemane, and told them to sit down and wait while he went on ahead to pray. He took Peter with him and Zebedee's two sons James and John, and began to be filled with anguish and despair.

Then he told them, "My soul is crushed with horror and sadness to the point of death . . . stay here . . . stay awake with me."

He went forward a little, and fell face downward on the ground, and prayed, "My Father! If it is possible, let this cup be taken away from me. But I want your will, not mine."

Then he returned to the three disciples and found them asleep. "Peter," he called, "couldn't you even stay awake with me one hour? Keep alert and pray. Otherwise temptation will overpower you. For the spirit indeed is willing, but how weak the body is!"

Matthew 26:36–41 LB

Feelings _____

[Jesus says] "I am leaving you with a gift—peace of mind and heart! And the peace I give isn't fragile like the peace the world gives. So don't be troubled or afraid. Remember what I told you—I am going away, but I will come back to you again. If you really love me, you will be very happy for me, for now I can go to the Father, who is greater than I am."

John 14:27, 28 LB

Feelings _____

[Paul says] I always thank God when I am praying for you, dear Philemon, because I keep hearing of your love and trust in the Lord Jesus and in his people. . . . . I myself have gained much joy and comfort from your love, my brother, because your kindness has so often refreshed the hearts of God's people.

Philemon 1:4–7 LB

Feelings _____

When Ahab told Queen Jezebel what Elijah had done, and that he had slaughtered the prophets of Baal, she sent this message to Elijah: "You killed my prophets, and now I swear by the gods that I am going to kill you by this time tomorrow night."

So Elijah fled for his life; he went to Beer-sheba, a city of Judah, and left his servant there. Then he went on alone into the wilderness, traveling all day, and sat down under a broom bush and prayed that he might die. "I've had enough," he told the Lord. "Take away my life. I've got to die some-time, and it might as well be now."

1 Kings 19:1–4 LB

Feelings _____

These verses show us that the Lord Jesus and others in the Bible were not afraid to show what they were feeling. In fact, in Matthew 4:1–11 Jesus shares with His friends about a time when Satan tried to tempt Him. No one else was there, and if Jesus hadn't thought it was a good thing to tell those close to Him about His struggles, we wouldn't know about this time in Jesus' life.

James (who many believe was Jesus' brother) says, "Admit your faults to one another and pray for each other so that you may be healed . . ." (James 5:16 LB).

Together Before God

Leader: Pause after each suggestion for prayer, giving everyone a chance to speak aloud. With eyes closed, and perhaps kneeling in a circle or holding hands:

1. Thank the Lord for the "good" feelings you have had this week. Do this aloud.

2. Now, ask Him to help with any of the "bad" feelings such as anger, jealousy, hurt feelings, loneliness, and so on, which you have had this week.

3. Ask God to forgive you and heal you, and then thank Him for His promise that He will do this in Jesus' name.

9 Special Because We Hear and Care

Where We Are Going

In this session we want to learn that caring for someone means *listening* to him and trying to meet his needs. We want to understand that we can listen to things besides just a person's words. We can listen with ears, eyes, and with our hearts, which are the "spiritual ears" that God gives us.

What We Will Need

- Pair of listening ears, listening eyes
- A pen or pencil
- A listening heart

FAMILY SHARING

Going around in a circle, guess what you think would be the person's (to your left) answers to the questions below. After you *guess* at his or her answers, have him or her tell what the real answers are.

1. What was the best time you had this year? (For small children, tie this into some time that they will remember, such as: "since school started" or "since Christmas." First person to leader's left guesses at what leader's answer will be. Then leader tells his real answer and so on around the circle.

2. What was your biggest disappointment or saddest day this year?

3. If you could spend the day with anyone (outside of the people here in this room) who would it be?

Did everyone guess the right answers for everyone else? Most likely not. It is surprising to learn that often we *guess* at what others around us think and want instead of *asking* them and listening for their answer.

In a way, we're like the frog and the barn swallow who became friends. . . . The swallow felt so warm towards his friend, the frog, that he invited him to live with him in the hanging mud nest on the wall of the cliff next to the river.

They found, however, that there really wasn't room for both of them in the nest, so the frog, deeply moved by his friend's generosity, insisted that the swallow sleep on his beautiful lily pad at the edge of the water while he took the nest.

All through the night the frog tossed and turned. The twigs in the bottom of the nest scratched his skin, which felt dry and uncomfortable so far from the water. Every now and then he heard the buzz of a mosquito flying by outside, but by the time he got his long tongue out the entrance of the nest, the insect was gone. He was hungry and thirsty, and sore from the difficult climb up the cliff.

The bird, meanwhile, tried to settle down on the lily pad. The rocking motion of the water made him feel most insecure, not to mention seasick. He would almost fall asleep—when a ripple of water would roll over his perch, wetting him to his underwings and chilling him thoroughly. Now and then a mosquito buzzed by, but as the swallow didn't have a long tongue, and was used to catching his insect meals in flight, the mosquito was the only one to get a bite.

This miserable arrangement went on night after night. And each morning the swallow would say, "Don't you *love* sleeping in my beautiful nest, safe up on the cliff?"

The frog, not wanting to hurt his friend's feelings, would reply, "Oh, yes, and don't you *love* my cool, wet lily pad?"

"Oh, yes," said the bird. But each day the *oh, yes* became more and more faint and the circles under the friends' eyes became more and more dark.

Then one night as the frog tossed and turned in his scratchy bed, he had a thought which he couldn't keep until morning.

"Swallow," he called into the night, "are you awake?"

"Yes," replied his friend, "I am too cold and wet to sleep."

The frog went on excitedly, "Every morning you ask me if I love sleeping in your nest. Could it be that you are saying *you* love sleeping in it?"

"Oh, yes!" answered Swallow. "And when *you* ask *me* if I love your lily pad are *you* saying that *you* love it?"

"Oh, yes!" shouted Frog.

"Then perhaps," said the bird, "we should trade back."

"Oh, yes!" shouted Frog, and they did.

Moral: What is lily pad for Frog may not be nest for Swallow (or vice versa), but they'll never know it unless they tell each other.

Questions

1. What do you think would have happened if Frog hadn't asked Swallow if he loved his nest?
2. What if Frog's feelings had been hurt, or he became angry because Swallow didn't like sleeping on his pad?
3. Do we have ways that keep people around us from telling us what they really want?

We can see that we owe those around us two things:

First: Be honest about what pleases us.

Second: Try to "hear" what the other person wants, even if he doesn't come right out and say it.

The Bible tells us that sometimes we purposely don't hear—as in this part about those who chose not to believe that Jesus is the One sent from God:

> . . . You will hear and see but not understand, for your hearts are too fat and your ears don't listen and you have closed your eyes against understanding, for you don't want to see and hear and understand and turn to me to heal you.

> Acts 28:26, 27 LB

God's Word tells us that we can *decide* to hear. Here are some other things to remember when we want those around us to be free to share with us. Read this passage aloud and write a list of things that will help you to be a hearing, caring member of your family:

> Love is very patient and kind, never jealous or envious, never boastful or proud, never haughty or selfish or rude. Love does not demand its own way. It is not irritable or touchy. It does not hold grudges and will hardly even notice when others do it wrong. It is never glad about injustice, but rejoices whenever truth wins out. If you love someone you will be loyal to him no matter what the cost. You will always believe in him, always expect the best of him, and always stand your ground in defending him.

> 1 Corinthians 13:4–7 LB

"HEARING, CARING" TIPS FOR US

Together Before God

Take a few minutes to close your eyes and be quiet together while each one thinks of ways he or she needs help in keeping these things in mind with others in the family. Maybe you need to ask God to help you not to be rude or irritable. One by one, ask God aloud to do this.

Unit 3

LIVING THINGS GROW

10 We Were All Small

11 Keeping the Windmills of Our Minds Oiled

12 Good News and Bad News

13 Faith Is a Living Thing

■■

10 We Were All Small

■■

Where We Are Going

During the past few weeks we have been discussing how important each of us is and how special our family is. Today we start a new series to learn just how we have grown. Since we are living creatures, we are constantly growing and changing. In this chapter we will talk about our beginning life and what has happened so far. (A note to parents: If you care to use this chapter as a jumping off spot for sex education it will be easy to do so.)

What We Will Need

- Additional sheets of paper for personal notebooks
- Baby pictures of each member of the family
- Recent pictures of each person
- Seeds, such as a package of flower seeds
- A picture of a flower, or a real one
- Pencils
- Several kinds of cheese, crackers, and fresh fruit for the treat

FAMILY SHARING

YOU ARE A MIRACLE!

Scientists know exactly what chemicals, cells, and tissues make up man. But they cannot make man. Man cannot make another man, only God can create such a miracle. In fact, man cannot even make a leaf or develop a rose.

LIFE IS A GIFT OF GOD!

God not only created the original garden and the original man—but He also provided the means so that life could be duplicated time and time again throughout history.

Have someone read the following questions, and write the answers in the space following:

61

1. How do we get new life in our gardens? When you are ready to plant a new flower garden, what do you do?

2. Your leader will now give each of you a little seed to hold. That little brown seed with no special character, will someday be a beautiful flower. After you plant that seed, what will it need in order to grow?

Let's say that next spring you have a beautiful red zinnia (or yellow marigold or pink snapdragon) from that little seed. You can see that it has many petals, a stem, leaves, roots, and a stamen (for the male) and a pistil (for the female), and pollen, that yellow powder that you can see on most flowers. The pollen must be carried from the stamen to the pistil and God has even supplied the means of transportation. Wind, insects, water, and birds do this for the flowers. Then more seeds are produced and next year you can have many, many flowering plants if you take care of the seeds properly now.

Now look at a real flower or a picture of a flower. Isn't it amazing that we can have something so beautiful from a tiny little seed!

Did you know that animals also come from tiny little seeds called eggs. And so did you!

You first began when a tiny little egg about the size of a pencil dot, or maybe the size of the period at the end of this sentence, joined with another microscopic cell called a sperm and you became an embryo. That word means your earliest stage of development before you were born. During this time you changed from an egg to looking like a real person—all this happened in just nine months.

3. What do you call little people when they are first born?

When you came as a baby, you had a lot of help being born. Not only did you have your mother and father, but you also had doctors and nurses to welcome you. Your parents saw you for the first time and you looked a lot different than you do today. You were given a name—you were a person!

Your leader will now give you paper to go into your personal scrapbook. You will start a story about yourself with your parents helping to fill in the details. (*Note to parents:* If you have small children, write this for them.)

4. At the top of the page write the title I WAS ONCE SMALL. Then complete each of the following:

I was born on:
The time was:
I weighed:
I was how long?
What were the doctors' names?
Why did my parents chose my name?
Some things my parents remember about me when I first arrived to be a member of this family are:

This is what I looked like: (*Parents:* Supply your children with a baby picture.) Paste the picture in your scrapbook.
What kind of food did I first like?
When did I first crawl and walk?
What were my first words?

5. What kind of a person were you when you were a toddler? Ask your parents to describe you.

   Did I talk a lot?
   Did I walk fast?
   Did I get into a lot of things?
   What was my favorite toy?
   Who was my favorite person?
   What was the cutest or funniest thing I did?

6. What do *you* remember about being little?

   What nice times do you remember?
   What funny things do you remember?
   What birthdays do you remember?
   What friends do you remember?
   Do you remember your favorite song when you were little?
   What was it?

7. What were your first school experiences?

   When did you start school?
   Who was your first teacher?
   What was the first thing you remember learning at school?
   Who were your school friends?

8. Where are you now?

   How old are you now?
   What grade are you in at school?
   Who are your favorite people?
   What is your favorite food?
   What one thing do you like doing more than any other?
   What is your favorite story or book?

You have really grown. Just look at all the ways you have changed since you were a tiny baby. You look different, you act differently and you can even think on your own.

Now paste a recent picture of yourself in your scrapbook. If you do not have one, ask your parents to take one of you so that you can have it for your permanent record of growth.

Just as a seed from a plant needs special care, in order to grow into a healthy plant, so do you.

9. What do you need in order to grow into a strong, healthy adult? Name some things and write them here. (Do this together.)

Do you know what you need to eat every day to keep healthy? The United States Department of Agriculture has published a statement that should be of help to all of us in eating a balanced diet:

MILK—for the average adult two or more cups per day. Children should have even more.

MEAT—two or more servings per day. (Any meats, egg, cheese, dried peas, beans, or nuts are included in this list.)

VEGETABLES AND FRUITS—four or more servings a day. At least one of these should be a citrus fruit, and a dark green or yellow vegetable.

BREAD AND CEREAL—four or more servings per day. These can be whole grain, enriched, or restored flour.

10. What else does your body need every day? Write your answers here:

Do you know that you are not the only person living in your body? Have someone read the following:

> Haven't you yet learned that your body is the home of the Holy Spirit God gave you, and that he lives within you? Your own body does not belong to you. For God has bought you with a great price. So use every part of your body to give glory back to God, because he owns it.
>
> 1 Corinthians 6:19, 20 LB

11. Who lives within you? _____

12. Just as our homes need to be kept nice, so do our bodies. What can we do to make the home of the Holy Spirit nicer? Write your answers here:

Your body is constantly growing and changing. Even when you are asleep, much is happening: Your heart continues to beat on the average of 72–80 (a child's slightly more) per minute, pumping about 2,500 gallons of blood each day; you continue to breathe 16–20 times per minute; and even your brain continues to work (as in dreams). The machinery of your body is always working. But it takes good care to keep it in working condition.

13. Here is a checklist. Ask yourself the following questions:

- Do I get the proper food in the proper amounts?
- Do I get enough rest?
- Do I get enough exercise?
- Do I get enough fresh air and water?
- Have I learned to relax and not worry? Did you know that our bodies were not made to worry—God tells us many, many times to just trust Him and not be anxious. (See Philippians 4:6 and 1 Peter 5:7.)

Together Before God

Bow your heads and have one person pray for all. Thank God for your bodies and for the growth that you have each had. Then ask Him to help you care for the temple of the Holy Spirit, to give you the strength and common sense to care for your bodies properly. And ask Him to help you not to worry, but to learn to trust in His care.

FAMILY FUN

Before you leave this family circle, do the following exercises and try (either as a family or on your own) to do these each day:

1. Stand on your toes and stretch one hand at a time as far as you can. Reach, reach, reach for the ceiling. Repeat 20 times. Then reach, reach, reach for the floor, bending from your waist, relaxing as much as possible.
2. Jog in place 50 times.
3. Now lie on the floor on your back. Put your clasped hands under your neck and pull your head up as if you were doing a sit-up, only go about halfway, then go back down flat. Do this 10 times.

A VERY IMPORTANT NOTE: If you have back or heart problems, please do not do any exercises without first seeing your doctor.

A FAMILY TREAT

Maybe this treat can be on Dad. Sit around the table and have a cheese-and-fruit party. Dad can buy a few kinds of cheese and fruit, along with crackers, put them on a tray and everyone can help himself. This treat is a really healthy one for you.

11 Keeping the Windmills of Our Minds Oiled

Where We Are Going

Our intellect and emotions are just as much a part of us as our bodies are, and they also need nutrition and growth. This session deals with what our intellect is and how we can best stretch our minds.

What We Will Need

- Pencils
- Items for No. 6
- Dictionary

FAMILY SHARING AND FAMILY FUN

When God created us, He not only created our bodies, but He also gave us minds so that we can think and reason and remember, and He gave us emotions so that we can have all kinds of feelings. All three parts are working within us every minute.

1. Have someone read the following list and everyone help decide which of the three columns each should be written in. Then have someone write each in its proper place.

   Writing a poem
   Being afraid because you've had a bad dream

Mopping the kitchen floor
Crying
Jumping up and down
Counting to *ten* in Spanish
Painting a picture
Spelling *supercalifragilisticexpialidocious*
Blinking your eyes
Singing the National Anthem
Remembering someone's name
Riding a bicycle
Laughing at a joke

PHYSICAL   **INTELLECTUAL**   **EMOTIONAL**

Now be careful—really think about these. Do you know that every one of these items involves your physical and intellectual functions, and some of them involve your emotions.

You are a very complicated machine. Whatever you do physically, you first have to think about, even though you are not always aware that you are thinking about it. Let's say you want to jump up and down. Before your feet can jump, they have to receive a little message from your brain telling them what to do. Now let's say you want to write a poem to someone you love.

First you experience the emotion of love and then your mind creates the words of the poem and again sends its little message to your hand to pick up the pen and start writing. And when you eat popcorn, you first feel hungry for it, you take it in your hands, and the little messages are sent to your mouth to open and close and eat. Your mind is something like a computer. You can program it and then it will produce. Now you don't have to stop and think about each step of eating, but that was programmed into your mind as a baby. It is now automatic and a habit. It just happens without any conscious thought now.

Your emotions also work closely with your physical functions. When you feel an emotion like fear, your body muscles get tight and tense. In fact, your heart even beats faster and pumps more blood through your body. So you can see that if you are going to be a healthy, whole person, each part of you has to be healthy.

2. What is an intellect? If you like, why don't you see what the dictionary has to say about this word. Write your answers here:

3. Let's all think of ten things we do with our intellect. Just call out your answers and have someone write them here:

(1)

(2)

(3)

(4)

(5)

(6)

(7)

(8)

(9)

(10)

4. What would happen to your body muscles if you just sat in a chair and didn't move for a week or so? Write here.

5. What happens to your thinking muscles if you just don't use them? Write here.

You become intellectually slow and stiff and boring! We need to grow intellectually just as we do with our bodies. When you are forced to learn in school, then it is easy to grow. But when you are out of school, it becomes difficult if you have not formed a learning habit in your life. It is necessary for each person to decide on his own to learn and stretch with your minds each day.

6. Each person right now think of one subject you would like to know more about. Sign your name in the space below along with the subject you would like to learn. Let me give you a couple of hints: Maybe you would like to learn a foreign language (there are records and books that you can purchase to use at home and special classes in most communities). Or maybe you have a desire to explore the life and habits of some animal; or how to tell the ages of trees; or learn to play the piano; or become acquainted with an historical figure through some books. Whatever it is, reach for that goal. You may even have to plan a family night at the public library in order to do this. If so, discuss when you will go and write that at the top of the list.

SIGN-UPS

Before your next session begins, go around the group and have each person give a little progress report on how he is doing with his new subject.

Psychiatrists tell us that everything we put into our minds, remains there on a shelf to be used at another time. This is what they call the sub-conscious mind.

If we fill our minds with negative, mean, ugly, useless, wrong thoughts, they will be the ones taking up the space in the cupboards of our minds. But if we think beautiful, healthy thoughts we can cram those cupboards full and know that someday, those things will be helpful to us. The things that we program into our human computer brain will be what eventually comes out.

The Bible has something very important to say about thinking. Have someone read these verses:

Finally, brethren, whatever is true, whatever is honorable, whatever is just, whatever is pure, whatever is lovely, whatever is gracious, if there is any excellence, if there is anything worthy of praise, think about these things.

Philippians 4:8 RSV

For as he thinketh in his heart, so is he. . . .

Proverbs 23:7 KJV

Together Before God

As a child in Sunday school I was taught a little prayer that was actually a prayer of King David. Will you all now bow your heads and have one person pray about thought-life and the things that we learn. Then will you all repeat together this little prayer:

Let the words of my mouth and the meditation of my heart be acceptable in thy sight, O Lord, my rock and my redeemer.

Psalms 19:14 RSV

12 Good News and Bad News

Where We Are Going

Emotions are part of life. Sometimes these experiences are fun, sometimes happy, and sometimes sad. Emotions can go from one extreme to the other. What are the emotions—and how can we handle them?

What We Will Need

- A timer or clock
- Paper
- Pencils

FAMILY SHARING

Have you ever seen a comedian on television begin his act by saying, "I have good news and I have bad news. First, the good news. . . ."? Ken and Miji Working's son Jeffrey recently started his day like that. He woke them early one morning and said:

> Dad and Mom, I have good news and I have bad news! First, the good news: I feel really great and it is such a beautiful day. And the bad news is: I just saw my bus pull away from the corner!

That's the way life is! Days can bring really good news and they can bring really sad news. And we all react with our emotions—we are either happy or sad. God knows that there are times that we have good news and bad news. Listen to what is said about that in the Bible:

> A time to cry;
> A time to laugh;
> A time to grieve;
> A time to dance.

Ecclesiastes 3:4 LB

Emotions are part of our personalities and something we each have. Sometimes you have heard someone describe another by saying, "Oh, she is such an emotional person." Well, we are all emotional people, but we choose to display our emotions in many different ways.

1. What kind of emotion are you capable of feeling? Go around the group and each person share some feeling he has had lately. Write the answers here:

We all express different emotions even to the same subject. As an example, if I say the word *fire* someone might respond with, "Oh, that makes me feel warm and cozy because I see myself sitting in front of a fireplace with the smell of roasted marshmallows permeating the room." The person next to the warm-and-cozy-feeling one might say, "Oh, fire makes me fearful because I think of a forest fire raging out of control." It is the same way with a word like *rain*. Someone might say, "Oh, I feel refreshed when it rains because I know that all the earth is getting watered, and I love to walk in the rain and let the drops splash on my face." The next person might say, "I feel depressed when it rains—everything is so gray and the roads are unsafe to travel!"

See what I mean? Now is your chance to be honest with your feelings. Let's just play a little game to understand how we can each react to the same word with our different emotions. Your leader will say the following words, and each person tell how you *feel* (not think) about each one. If it will help you *feel* the words better, just close your eyes and imagine that you are experiencing these right now. This is not a test to be corrected—there are *no* right or wrong answers. Any emotion you feel will be acceptable.

2. Your leader will say the following:

   Airplanes
   Bath
   Garbage trucks
   Football games
   Naps
   Mouse
   Dolls
   Work
   Spinach
   Reading

Emotions are the feelings we have inside of us—but they produce actions on the outside. If you feel depressed, you act one way. If you feel happy, you act another way.

3. How do you act when you are depressed? Write some answers here:

4. When you feel happy, how do you act? Write your answers here:

5. How do you think your emotions make other people feel? Write down some ideas:

Have someone read the following:

© 1963 United Feature Syndicate, Inc.

6. If you were Charlie Brown or Linus, how would you react to Lucy's crabby nature? Write some ideas:

7. If you were Charlie Brown or Linus (or maybe Lucy's parents), how could you help her to stop being a crabby person before she gets to be a "crabby old woman"? Write some answers here:

8. If you were Lucy, how could you change your crabbiness? Write here:

9. Do you think that it is important for people who have a set pattern or habit of bad moods to make changes in their emotional actions? Write down your ideas:

There are times in each life when we can and should express our emotions with a "bad mood" because that is the way we feel. And we have to accept and help each other at times like that, as long as it is not an everyday occurrence. The Bible says something about that, too:

Share each other's troubles and problems, and so obey our Lord's command.

Galatians 6:2 LB

10. How can we help each other and share each other's trouble and problems? Write your answers here:

Have someone read this verse: "Rejoice with those who rejoice, weep with those who weep" (Romans 12:15 RSV).

Will you read that verse again, please.

Do you know what I have noticed about us and the way we treat others? If someone goes to a friend with a big problem, the friend is usually willing to "weep" with the person. But—if some really wonderful thing happens to someone, what emotions usually come glaring out of our personalities?

11. What do you think happens? Write your answer here:

Did you say *jealousy?* Well, it is true!

12. Can you think of a time when you have had such an experience? Will you share this with your family?

Have someone read the following verse:

Love is very patient and kind, never jealous or envious, never boastful or proud. . . .

1 Corinthians 13:4 LB

Psychologists try to train people to be *appropriate* with their emotions. That is also what the verse in Romans says, too. It does *not* say: "Rejoice with those who weep, and weep with those who rejoice."

13. If you are feeling really terrible about something, and someone says, "Oh, come on, that's nothing!" How do you feel toward that person? Discuss.

Let's consider another question about emotions. Do we express the right kind of emotion? We need an emotional balance in our lives. If we "go all to pieces" over something really small, that is not being balanced. For example, does a glass of orange juice spilled at the breakfast table destroy your good mood for the day? If so, that emotion is inappropriate. We should be able to accept and forget minor annoyances. However, if you have just heard some really sad news, it would be inappropriate to *laugh it off.*

Have you ever felt that something was wrong with your emotions? I'm sure you have, because at times everyone feels emotionally drained or imbalanced. Let me just give you some reasons that I have known for being depressed for a long period of time:

- **Not feeling any self-worth:**   (You may want to review the first section of this book.)
- **Physical problems:**   Physical problems can cause emotional problems just as emotional problems can cause physical disorders. When this happens, it is wise to see a doctor and get a checkup.
- **Improper diet and lack of sleep:**   Our children are in nursery school and first grade. Both the principal and the director of the schools recently sent home notes with all the children, asking the parents to be sure that their children are getting enough rest and eating nutritious food. The children who do not have these things are depressed and sluggish at school and are not doing their best work.
- **Misdirected emotional outbursts:**   If you are angry at yourself or the whole world, why not take your frustrations out on a tennis court or some other form of exercise, rather than be mad at your family.
- **Lack of order and balance in your life:**   If you are always disorganized and late, you are probably in a bad mood frequently.
- **Not saying when something is bothering you.**
- **Not having a relationship with God:**   He is interested in the whole person and will help you to know your self-worth and value, help you set goals and directions, and fill your life with love.

14. If you are physically ill, who do you see? Write it down:

15. If you are emotionally ill, who should you see? Write it down:

It is true that when you have a physical problem, you see a doctor. And when you have an emotional problem, you should see a trained specialist, as well. God has given different talents and gifts to different people. To some He has given the talent of healing or curing people. If you feel that you want to talk with someone about your emotions, call your doctor, minister, or a trained psychologist. To seek help may be the smartest thing that you have ever done. It can help you get your life in order and your priorities straightened out.

Together Before God

Bow your heads and for just a quiet moment study your emotions right now. Ask God in the quietness of your own heart to help you grow emotionally and become mature. Thank God for the variety of feelings that you experience. Ask Him to help you be honest with your feelings and to know how to use them for your good and the good of those you love. Let one person close the prayer time together.

FAMILY FUN

This session closes with a time of *charades*—that means a game where you act out some titles. Today choose song titles. Give every person an assignment and a turn to act out the song. *Leader* will chose songs that express emotions. Write the titles on small slips of paper and hand them out, giving the easiest ones to the smallest children. Some suggestions are: "Cry Me a River," "Let a Smile Be Your Umbrella," "I Feel Pretty," "Funny Girl," "People Who Need People."

■■

13 Faith Is a Living Thing

■■

Where We Are Going

In this lesson we will attempt to help your family understand that our faith is alive, to discover when it was born, and to discuss ways that it can grow and what we can do to help its growth.

What We Will Need

- Pencils or pens
- Paper for interviewing
- Tape recorder (optional)

FAMILY SHARING

If you fly into Los Angeles on a clear day, it is really interesting to look down on the miles and miles of houses, sitting side by side. You are aware of strange little blue punctuation marks over all the terrain of Southern California. Those little blue dots represent a way of life for many residents of Southern California—they are swimming pools. We also have one in our backyard and during the months between April and October we spend many hours every week in the pool with our children and guests. Along with the laughter, fun and exercise, comes an added amount of work for pool owners, however. The pool has to be cleaned about twice a week. Last year, we began noticing that our pool had formed little black dots along the edge of the tile and we couldn't seem to get it cleared up. We called in a local expert to tell us what the problem was. He checked the water and reported: "Your pool water is dead."

"Dead?" we asked—"How does water become dead?" Well it seems that when a pool is filled, the water circulates from the pool, through the filter, then the heater and pump, and back into the pool. This goes on day after day, week after week. Our pool had the same water circulating for about three years. It was worn out and the chemicals were no longer effec-

tive and because of that, the little black dots that were forming were algae. The water still looked good and inviting, but it was dead and not pure. So the pool had to be drained and fresh water had to be put back into the pool. Our pool water is now alive and the only little creatures thriving are our children.

Sometimes we humans are just like pools containing dead water. We circulate the same way as Christians with a living faith but we discover that sinful algae are growing in our lives. The things like doubt, jealousy, gossiping, and hate are taking away from the beauty that we could have in our lives.

1. Can you name some other things that are permitted to grow in lives that are not made pure by Christ? Write your answers here:

But Christ has offered something more for us. Have someone read the following:

He replied, "If you only knew what a wonderful gift God has for you, and who I am, you would ask me for some *living* water!". . . . "But the water I give them," he said, "becomes a perpetual spring within them, watering them forever with eternal life."

John 4:10–14 LB

2. What or who do you think is the *living water* that we receive from Christ? Write the answer:

Have someone read:

. . . For you are God's temple, the home of the living God, and God has said of you, "I will live in them and walk among them, and I will be their God and they shall be my people."

2 Corinthians 6:16 LB

. . . "I am the resurrection and the life; he who believes in me, though he die, yet shall he live, and whoever lives and believes in me shall never die. . . ."

John 11:25 26 RSV

3. Who gives us this life? Write here:

4. What makes our faith living? Write:

5. There are many, many religions of this world. Can you name any that claim to believe in a living God or one that offers to fill its followers with life? Write:

6. State in just a few words what you think faith is. Write your answers:

7. Let's see what the Bible says about faith. Have someone read:

   What is faith? It is the confident assurance that something we want is going to happen. It is the certainty that what we hope for is waiting for us, even though we cannot see it up ahead.

   Hebrews 11:1 LB

   Now put in your own words what you think faith is:

Just as your physical life begins at a certain time, so does your spiritual life.

    8. *Everyone:* Call out your own birthday.
    9. Do any of you recall when your *spiritual* birthday was? Discuss.

You may not even remember when your faith-life began, and that is fine. It doesn't mean that you have no faith—after all, no one remembers the actual experience of being born and you still have life.

At the time your faith began it might have been no greater than just a recognition of Christ and who He is. You perhaps didn't feel any great power. Let's see what the Bible says about *little faith.*

    . . . . I say to you, if you have faith as a grain of mustard seed, you will say to this mountain, "Move hence to yonder place," and it will move; and nothing will be impossible to you.

Matthew 17:20 RSV

Can you see that you don't have to start your spiritual life as a giant. You start as a baby. And just as physical babies grow, so will spiritual babies.

    10. Why do spiritual babies need to grow? Write your ideas:

Now have someone read the following verses:

Like newborn babes, long for the pure spiritual milk, that by it you may grow up to salvation; for you have tasted the kindness of the Lord.

1 Peter 2:2, 3 RSV

    11. Physical babies are born into families. So are spiritual babies. What is the family of a spiritual baby? Write:

We as families help each other. When babies are little they are completely cared for by their parents—then they become a little bit more independent. They crawl, then they walk, and then they fall.

12. How do parents respond when a baby falls? Write:

13. How do you think God responds to us when we stumble and fall? Write:

14. How should we treat each other when we see a member of our family take a step in faith and then stumble? Write:

15. How does faith grow? Have someone read the following verses before answering this question:

But grow in the grace and knowledge of our Lord and Savior Jesus Christ. . . .

2 Peter 3:18 RSV

Him we proclaim, warning every man and teaching every man in all wisdom, that we may present every man mature in Christ.

Colossians 1:28 RSV

Now answer:

To help you remember how we as Christians grow, here's a little formula:

CHRISTIAN MATURITY = KOINONIA (that special relationship that includes God) + KNOWLEDGE OF CHRIST.

Or . . . CM = K + KC

16. When you meet someone new, how can you build a relationship with that person? Can you ever build a relationship with anyone, if you do not spend time with him or her?

17. How can we get to know Jesus Christ? How can we spend time with Him?

FAMILY FUN

Your leader will give you paper (or a little notebook) and a pencil. Pretend you are a newspaper reporter, a host of a television talk show, or any interviewer. Select a person outside your family, who has an exciting, living faith. Call the person and make an appointment to talk with him or her. It might be your grandmother, an uncle, a teacher, your minister, or a neighbor. (Parents: If you have small children, do the interviewing together. Decide together who to call and then combine your efforts.) Ask questions that will help you understand that person's faith—such as:

- How long have you known Christ?
- When did you first discover God's love for you?
- What one experience have you had that has helped to strengthen your faith?
- Has any one person been a strong influence in your life in helping you know Christ better? Who and how?
- What do you do in your life to help your faith grow?
- What advice would you give me to help me grow?

In about a week, have your report ready to give at a dinner hour, or sometime when the family is all together.

Unit 4

AT HOME IN THE WORLD

14 God Made It for Us

15 He Left It in Our Hands

16 *In* But Not *Of*

17 Ambassadors of God

■■■

14 God Made It for Us

■■■

Where We Are Going

We would like to become more aware of God's gifts to us—this world, nature, and our five senses. We hope to expand our capacity for appreciation. This lesson could be subtitled "Nature Appreciation."

What We Will Need

- Pencils
- A box for your Treasure Chest or . . .
- Several magazines for cutting
- Scotch tape or thumb tacks
- Scissors
- A Bible

Note to Leader: If you are to take a walk as suggested in FAMILY FUN, you will want to do this session during the daylight hours.

FAMILY SHARING

1. Have someone read the following verses and then answer the questions:

> The heavens belong to the Lord, but he has given the earth to all mankind.
>
> Psalms 115:16 LB

> For Jehovah created the heavens and earth and put everything in place, and he made the world to be lived in, not to be an empty chaos.
>
> Isaiah 45:18 LB

Who made the world?

Who was the world made for?

Have a good reader read the following short story:

I have often thought it would be a blessing if each human being were stricken blind and deaf for a few days at some time during his early adult life. Darkness would make him more appreciative of sight. Silence would teach him the joys of sound.

Now and then I have tested my seeing friends to discover what they see. Recently I asked a friend, who had just returned from a long walk in the woods, what she had observed. "Nothing in particular," she replied.

How was it possible, I asked myself, to walk for an hour through the woods and see nothing worthy of note? I, who cannot see, find hundreds of things to interest me through mere touch. I feel the delicate symmetry of a leaf. I pass my hands lovingly about the smooth skin of a silver birch, or the rough shaggy bark of a pine. In spring I touch the branches of trees hopefully in search of a bud, the first sign of awakening nature after her winter's sleep. Occasionally, if I am very fortunate, I place my hand gently on a small tree and feel the happy quiver of a bird in full song.

That story was written by Helen Keller, who could neither see nor hear.

2. Have you ever taken a walk and not noticed "anything of note"?

We are all guilty of taking beauty for granted. Let's try to become more aware of the beauty around us. When God gave us a gift of nature and the world, He was not at all monotonous with His Creation. He used so much variety.

3. Take a few minutes now and list some of the scenes you can remember that show a variety of design, shape, color, and texture. For example: Think of a place you have seen that had different kinds of trees—perhaps a palm tree standing straight and tall near a gracefully bending weeping willow. List some of your favorite "scene memories" here:

4. Now using your five senses, what variety did God use to make you enjoy His gifts fully:

THINGS I LIKE TO . . .

SMELL _____

SEE _____

HEAR_____

TASTE_____

TOUCH _____

5. When you become good at anything, it takes practice. Some of us will really need to use practice on our senses of appreciation and awareness. Starting right now, let's make a practice of telling someone—or at least thinking—of some of God's gifts in nature that we really are aware of and that we can appreciate. Try to do this every day.

Go around the group and tell what one thing of nature and this world you most appreciate today. Write your items here:

FAMILY FUN

- Pretend that today is the first time that you have been able to see. Go for a short walk and each person find one thing of nature to put in your Treasure Chest of nature. Perhaps it can be a leaf with symmetric design or a rock. When you get back, share your "find" with the family and put it in the box. Leave the box out for a couple of days so that you can all be reminded of God's gifts to us. Or . . . .

- If the weather does not permit a walk in your area, take some magazines and each person find a picture that shows something of nature that you can appreciate. Cut out the pictures and share with the family. Post these someplace for a couple of days. You can just tape them to the refrigerator door for all to see. And/or . . . .

- Set the alarm early some morning and go to a place where you can clearly see the sunrise. Can you feel an excitement for the newness of life that God gives us each day?

■■■

15 He Left It in Our Hands

■■■

Where We Are Going

We want to stress in this chapter what our personal responsibility is for the *management* of God's gift to us—this world. What is expected from us?

What We Will Need

- Heavy construction paper
- Black felt-tipped pens
- Straight pins
- Supplies needed for the FAMILY FUN section

FAMILY SHARING

Have someone read the following (*italics* are added):

> And God said, Let us make man in our own image, after our likeness: and *let them have dominion over the fish of the sea, and over the fowl of the air, and over the cattle, and over all the earth, and over every creeping thing that creepeth upon the earth.*
>
> Genesis 1:26 KJV

> Then God said, "Let us make a man—someone like ourselves, *to be the master of all life upon the earth and in the skies and in the seas.*"
>
> Genesis 1:26 LB

1. What does it mean to "have dominion" over the earth? Write here:

After you have answered this question, go back to the above verse and have someone read it again, and in place of the words *have dominion* or *be the master* insert the words *be managers.*

2. Think of some managers that you know: the manager of the local supermarket, of a baseball team, of parks, banks, or theatres, and so on. You might think of this in terms of "supervisor" or "superintendent." What are some responsibilities of managers? What do they do? Write:

If we look around at our surroundings, it seems evident that we, as managers of the earth, sea and air, have not done a very good job:

- Some animals, birds, and fish are becoming extinct.
- Our lakes and streams are polluted and our fish are being poisoned.
- In many countries of the world, we have more people than space or food.
- Our natural resources are running low.
- Our economy is in a serious recession. We are making more money than ever before and still we cannot stretch it far enough.
- Our cities are plagued by smog and air pollution.
- Thousands of people are starving today because of lack of food.

3. Do you know what the word *ecology* means? Write down your definition here:

My definition is that it means the relationship between us and animals and our surrounding environment.

This world was created with order and balance, and we humans are asked to keep it that way. Just think about all of nature and how each part helps another part. For example, plant and animal life work together. Plants and trees produce oxygen necessary for our breathing, and animals in turn breathe out carbon dioxide which plants need for photosynthesis. And the pollination of plants is done by wind, insects, birds or water.

4. How do you use plants? Are they absolutely necessary for your survival? Listed on the next page are several boxes with uses for plants. At the bottom of the page are the names of many types of plants. Put these names in the correct boxes. Some can be used more than once. Add more names if you want to.

By now you have probably come to the conclusion that we need plants for survival. The Agriculture Extension Service of the University of California, Riverside campus, gives us the following important information regarding lawns: "Lawns are not only pretty to look at, nice to walk on, but essential for our good health. A 30-square-foot lawn supplies enough oxygen for a family of four."

Another area badly in need of some management is the area of waste, inflation, and economy. President Ford said that we Americans are known as "the world's worst wasters." We waste our natural resources, our food, our money, and we waste our time.

5. Now is your chance to be a really honest family. Go around the group and each person tell what you have noticed that is wasted in your home and life (without blaming or defending yourselves). Write them here:

PLANTS FOR FOOD

PLANTS FOR BEAUTY

PLANTS FOR CLOTHES

PLANTS FOR FURNITURE AND HOMES

PLANTS FOR COMFORT AND HEALTH

LIST IN THE RIGHT BOXES:

Banana tree, grapevine, grass, mint, cotton, redwood tree, daisy, cacao, coffee, peach tree, oak, maple, walnut, carnation, weeping willow, wheat, alfalfa, tomato, rose, jute plant, ivy, flax, sugarcane, castor-oil plant, foxglove (which produces digitalis), corn, bamboo, birch, pine, oregano, juniper, tulip, lemon, moss.

Have you considered little things like paper towels? Do you toss out clothes instead of mending them? Do you make more trips than is necessary with your car? Do you share books and magazines with your neighbors or a local hospital?

The Southern California Gas Company has an ad running on television that says:

> . . . if 20 percent of the homes in Southern California have leaky hot water faucets . . . the amount of energy wasted in a year is enough . . . to provide five-minute hot showers for every person in a city the size of Santa Monica . . . every day for over three years.

Now for the math experts in your house, here are some facts to help you figure out just how much water that is: The city of Santa Monica has a population of about 90,000 people. There are approximately 3,950,000 on the gas company lines. A shower head uses 5 gallons of water per minute. The average shower is 5 minutes long. Now that's a lot of water that we Southern Californians are wasting! I am sure that the same is true in your geographical area as well.

We Americans are not only wasteful, we are sloppy litterbugs! I am sure that you have seen people making a mess on the public streets, theatres, and ball parks just as I have.

Sesame Street television show has a lovable moppet named Oscar. He makes his home in a beat-up, dented trash can and complains about all the normal apartment dwellers who live on Sesame Street. He sings a funny little song entitled "I Love Trash," written by Jeffrey Moss:

> Oh, I love trash,
> Anything dirty or dingy or dusty,
> Anything ragged or rotten or rusty;
> Oh, I love trash!
>
> I have here a sneaker that's tattered and worn;
> It's all full of holes, and the laces are torn—
> A gift from my mother the day I was born.
> I love it because it's trash.
>
> I have here some newspaper, thirteen months old.
> I've wrapped fish inside it; it's smelly and cold;
> But I wouldn't trade it for a big pot of gold.
> I love it because it's trash.

I've a clock that won't work and an old telephone,
A broken umbrella, a rusty trombone,
And I am delighted to call them my own.
I love them because they're trash.

© 1970 Festival Attractions, Inc.

Maybe we should all be a little bit like Oscar and collect more trash. I'm sure that keeping it around in our homes is not the best place for it—but let's at least pick up papers and junk and put them where they belong—in your beat-up, dented trash cans. Wouldn't it be nice if *everyone* in your neighborhood took more pride in the way he kept his home and street! It can start with *you* and with your home and yard and maybe the Oscar Bug will become infectious in your neighborhood.

FAMILY FUN

Let's consider the areas of management that we have just discussed: PLANTS, ANIMALS, NATURAL RESOURCES, WASTEFULNESS.

1. Which of these areas would you like to manage? Take a piece of construction paper, cut in either a three-inch circle or rectangle. With a felt-tipped pen, write your name and area for management.

What to do with your area of management is the next problem. Discuss this as a family. You can decide on individual projects or on a family project. One idea is to replace an area that is now full of weeds with a garden (either flower or vegetable). Be sure to have the proper soil, food, water, and light. A second possibility is: Go through the house on a fix-it tour. Or: Plant a tree; help an elderly neighbor fix his yard; pick up all litter from your yard and street; find a home for a stray animal; share a report with your family on a threatened animal species. (You can talk with your librarian.)

2. Helpful reminders are accepted and needed in most of our homes. Are we in the habit of leaving on lights and televisions when we leave a room, or not eating all of our food? Make a game out of reminding people to be better guardians of what God has given to us. Do this in a nice way!

3. After you have completed your project for making this world nicer—why don't you treat yourselves to delicious ice-cream sundaes! Good managers deserve rewards.

16 *In* But Not *Of*

Where We Are Going

We must all live in this world subject to the same disappointments, sorrows, fear, happiness, and joy as our neighbors—but we have an advantage that some of our neighbors may not have. We have Christ's promise to be with us through the Comforter, the Holy Spirit.

What We Will Need

- A glove
- Art supplies—such as macaroni, spaghetti, beans, nails, straw, twigs, boards, old magazines
- Any good painting, print, or mosaic from your house
- Scissors

FAMILY SHARING

Have someone read the following verse:

The thief's purpose is to steal, kill and destroy. My purpose is to give life in all its fullness.

John 10:10 LB

I wanted to know what the word *fullness* meant, so I got out a dictionary and this is what I found. *Fullness* means abundance. And *abundant* means: present in great quantity; more than sufficient; overflowing; plentiful.

Life has many sides, colors, and shapes. I have heard people describe life by saying that it is like a great painting or mosaic—it has many dimensions. Your leader will now hold up a picture or painting for you to study for a couple of minutes.

1. Can you see different colors and shapes? Point out some of these.
2. If happiness could be described as a color, what color would you choose? Each person give your "happiness color" here:

3. If sadness could be described as a color, what color would you choose? Write the choices down:

4. If you were going to paint a great picture, could you do so by just using bright colors—or by just using dull colors?

Pictures, just like lives, are done with *happy* and *sad* colors. But since we know that God is the Painter of our lives, we can be assured that He will complete our lives with just the right colors and there will be a beautiful portrait in the end.

Have someone read the following verse:

And we know that all that happens to us is working for our good if we love God and are fitting into his plans.

Romans 8:28 LB

Take out crayons or paints now. On page 106 is a picture to which all should contribute—using both your *happy* and *sad* colors to complete it.

Every person who now lives or who has ever lived in history has had joys and sorrows, happiness and disappointments. You are not alone. But there is something else—or rather Some*one* else—to comfort us. Listen to what Jesus promises:

If you love me, you will keep my commandments. And I will pray the Father, and he will give you another Counselor to be with you for ever, even the Spirit of truth, whom the world cannot receive, because it neither sees him nor knows him; you know him, for he dwells with you, and will be in you.

John 14:15–17 RSV

Your leader will now place a glove in the center of the table. Everyone study this glove for a minute and then answer these questions.

5. Is that glove keeping any hand warm and protected right now?
6. Can that glove pick up an object right now?
7. Can that glove snap a finger right now?

I'm sure that you all said a very loud *no* to all three questions. Now have someone in the group put the glove on his or her hand. Go back to the above questions and see how you answer them now.

8. What made the difference between the first set of questions and the second? In many ways, we are just like that glove. Have someone read:

Yes, I am the Vine; you are the branches. Whoever lives in me and I in him shall produce a large crop of fruit. For apart from me you can't do a thing.

John 15:5 LB

Living our lives in this world is not always easy. There are some rough edges to be smoothed and some very dark times that we must work our way through, but we can do it because of the strength and power that is now within us.

Sometimes it helps us to get through the dark periods if we can share these times with others. And the bright times somehow seem even brighter if they are shared with those we love. Right now let's take just a couple of minutes to think about the sadness you may be feeling or the joy you may be experiencing.

9. Share these times with your family now. Be as honest and open as you can and then carefully listen to what the others are saying.

10. Can you help anyone else in your family right now, or can they help you? In what ways? Write some of them:

God promises to help us. Have someone read the following verses:

In everything you do, put God first, and he will direct you and crown your efforts with success.

Proverbs 3:6 LB

For I can do everything God asks me to with the help of Christ who gives me the strength and power.

Philippians 4:13 LB

But remember this—the wrong desires that come into your life aren't anything new and different. Many others have faced exactly the same problems before you. And no temptation is irresistible. You can trust God to keep the temptation from becoming so strong that you can't stand up against it, for he has promised this and will do what he says. He will show you how to escape temptation's power so that you can bear up patiently against it.

1 Corinthians 10:13 LB

I have told you all this so that you will have peace of heart and mind. Here on earth you will have many trials and sorrows; but cheer up, for I have overcome the world.

John 16:33 LB

Sometimes it happens that things that we think are very sad or negative are turned into beautiful, positive experiences. This doesn't mean that you will not have tears or experience real hurts, because you will. But even through the tears you can see a ray of hope and know that God is able to use even the tears. Yesterday was a gloomy, rainy day here in Los Angeles. But when we went out last night the clouds had moved on and the moon and stars were shining. Today is a sparkling day, because the rain washed the smog out of the air and the sidewalks and trees have all had a shower. To be outside today makes one happy to be alive. The rain had a real purpose yesterday and it is the same way with our tears and heartaches.

I have a very dear friend, Catherine, who has taught me and others much about turning sorrows into joy. Her four-year-old little boy developed a fatal blood disease. She recently shared with me her feelings during the time her child was ill. She remembers her happiness during that time. Do you know why? This is what she told me:

The doctor who had the painful job of telling us our son had a disease for which there was no known cure had an uncommon ability for telling the truth while not destroying all hope. He never put a time limit on our son's life, and I will be forever grateful for this fact. My initial reaction was disbelief, and then anger—feelings which I have since learned are quite common. But the important thing was that hope had not been destroyed, and with God's help I began to look for ways to make our little boy's life a happy one. I thanked God every morning for giving us another day to spend with him—and a strange thing happened. In the midst of pain I experienced much happiness and joy and a deep sense of appreciation for everything we were able to share with our son. For the first time in my life everything seemed to be in its proper perspective.

After and through her tears she experienced real joy. Her little boy did die and she was lonely. I am sure that even today when she thinks about him, she still misses him, for she loved him deeply. But God was with her and is still with her. During that period it seemed that God was using dark, sad colors in the mosaic of her life. But the picture He is creating is indeed beautiful. When she again began to see some sunshine in her life, she decided to help other families who were experiencing the same loss and hurt. She volunteered her time to work at Children's Hospital. Last year she taught teachers at a local college how best to help families who were faced with sickness and grief.

She didn't turn her sorrow into self-pity. She looked around her and, with God's strength in her life, reached out to others who hurt and were in need. God has given Catherine and Lester another son now. Days again are painted with bright colors—Kyle is a joy to his parents! The Master Artist has been at work in her life and the portrait is one of His masterpieces.

God will take our lives just as they are right now and create something wonderful. Our friend Bill Gaither has written a song that says that:

Something beautiful,
Something good;
All my confusion
He understood;
All I had to offer Him
Was brokenness and strife,
But He made something
Beautiful
Of my life.
© Copyright 1971 by William J. Gaither

God is now working on something beautiful for your lives. You can trust Him because He loves you and lives within you.

FAMILY FUN

We would like for you to make something beautiful out of "junk." You will be given all kinds of junk. Take complete freedom to make whatever you chose to make. Set the timer for about a half hour.

I'll give you a couple of ideas for junk art that we have in our house. Sitting on a shelf in our den is a piece of authentic junk art. My husband found it at an art show in Chicago several years ago. It is a man sitting at a grand piano. It is made with old nails, a battery part, a spark plug, an old sawed-off saw. A very imaginative mind saw some beauty in all the junk in his garage.

We also have a mosaic made by three-year-old Jonathan at his nursery school. It is a design made of macaroni that has been dyed different colors with food coloring. This is mounted on a plain white paper plate.

Stephen just gave me a mosaic cross and a rainbow. Both are made of little tiny pieces of tissue paper and glued to construction paper.

And I have done some nice things with ice-cream cartons. I picked up a few at a local ice-cream store and covered them with leftover wallpaper to match various rooms. It is easy to make a collage on them, too, and then spray them with a finish when they are dry.

■■

17 Ambassadors of God

■■

Where We Are Going

In order to be at home in the world we need to understand what our purpose and mission is to the world. What does God want us to be and do for our particular world or neighborhood?

What We Will Need

- Paper
- Pencil

FAMILY SHARING

Washington, D. C., as the capital of our country, welcomes many foreign residents. Many of these residents are representatives to our government from other countries of the world. And in return, we have representatives in the same countries. These special people are called ambassadors. When our President sends an ambassador to another country, he is asking that person to be his personal representative to that nation. The new ambassador and his family move to the new country and take our government embassy as their new home. The President is careful to select someone who can spread the goodwill of our country to the new nation. He tries to send someone who can be a friend to the people and help them understand the people of the United States of America. The embassy and grounds belong to the United States and the American flag flies overhead. To be chosen as an ambassador is a great honor.

1. What kind of a person do you think the President looks for when he must select someone to represent us to another country? Write your answers here:

2. What are some characteristics of friendship? Write:

3. What kind of knowledge of our country and the new country do you think the ambassador must have?

God has chosen you to be His ambassador to your particular neighborhood and circle of friends. Your home can really be His embassy on your street. You are an honored person!

Let's look at some ways God wants us to be His ambassadors: Have someone read the following verses and on the lines following each verse, tell how these show us how best to serve God:

You are the light of the world. A city set on a hill cannot be hid. Nor do men light a lamp and put it under a bushel, but on a stand, and it gives light to all in the house. Let your light so shine before men, that they may see your good works and give glory to your Father who is in heaven.

Matthew 5:14–16 RSV

4. God wants us to be a _____.

5. What does a light do? _____

_____.

Honor your father and mother, and, You shall love your neighbor as yourself.

Matthew 19:19 RSV

. . . "You shall love your neighbor as yourself." There is no other commandment greater than these.

Mark 12:31 RSV

6. God wants us to _____.

7. He also wants us to love_____.

8. How can we show love?_____

_____

_____.

Jesus says, "And I, when I am lifted up . . . will draw all men to myself" (John 12:32 RSV).

9. We are to lift up_____.

10. How can we "lift Jesus up"? _____

_____.

Rejoice with those who rejoice, weep with those who weep. Live in harmony with one another; do not be haughty, but associate with the lowly; never be conceited. Repay no one evil for evil. . . . If possible, so far as it depends upon you, live peaceably with all. . . . "If your enemy is hungry, feed him; if he is thirsty, give him drink;" . . . . Do not be overcome by evil, but overcome evil with good.

Romans 12:15–21 RSV

Let love be genuine; hate what is evil, hold fast to what is good; love one another with brotherly affection; outdo one another in showing honor. Never flag in zeal, be aglow with the Spirit, serve the Lord. Rejoice in your hope, be patient in tribulation . . . . practice hospitality.

Romans 12:9–13 RSV

11. From the above verses, write some other things that God wants us to do as His ambassadors.

Know that the Lord is God! It is he that made us, and we are his; we are his people, and the sheep of his pasture.

Psalms 100:3 RSV

12. God wants us to know _____.

In order to be effective ambassadors we have to have knowledge of God. Can you imagine what a bad job an ambassador of the United States would do if he didn't know anything about our country or our President?

Work hard so God can say to you, "Well done." Be a good workman, one who does not need to be ashamed when God examines your work. Know what his Word says and means.

2 Timothy 2:15 LB

13. We should study His work and know _____.

Let your speech always be gracious, seasoned with salt, so that you may know how you ought to answer every one.

Colossians 4:6 RSV

14. We should be able to _____.

So we are ambassadors for Christ, God making his appeal through us. We beseech you on behalf of Christ, be reconciled to God.

2 Corinthians 5:20 RSV

15. God wants to use us to appeal to others on behalf of Christ because Christ can _____.

Together Before God

An ambassador representing our country is commissioned by the President of the United States. You are commissioned by God. Together as a family will you accept this commission from God?

Many years ago, a great man of God wrote a prayer that you can take as your Prayer of Commission. Have a good printer copy this prayer and place it in a spot where all the ambassadors of your house will be able to read it often.

Please kneel in a circle, holding hands, and repeat the following prayer after your leader:

Lord, make me an instrument of thy peace,
Where there is hatred, let me sow love;
Where there is injury, pardon;
Where there is doubt, faith;
Where there is despair, hope;
Where there is darkness, light;
Where there is sadness, joy.

Oh divine Master, grant that I may not so much seek to be consoled as to console,
to be understood as to understand, to be loved as to love;
For it is in giving that we receive;
it is in pardoning that we are pardoned, it is in dying that we
are born to eternal life.   *The Prayer of St. Francis of Assisi*

FAMILY FUN

One of the chief roles of an ambassador is to be host of the embassy. He always invites a lot of people for dinner parties, teas, and so on. Do you remember what God said about entertaining, back in the verse you read in Romans 12:13? It was, "Practice hospitality."

Together now, decide how you want to entertain in God's embassy —your home. Can you invite a family from your neighborhood for dinner, or coffee and dessert, or maybe a Saturday-morning brunch? Think of a family that you would like to be friends with and that you would like to introduce (when the time is right) to Jesus. This is a family project, so—as a family —pray about this, decide on the details together, and work on this party together.

1. Whom will you invite?
2. When?
3. What kind of a party?
4. What will you serve?
5. Divide up the work—who will do what?

Be sure to remember that you are representing the Lord Jesus in your neighborhood.

Unit 5

BEING IN GOD'S FAMILY
IS SPECIAL

18 Special Because We Are Adopted

19 Special Because We Are Freed
     From Guilt

20 Special Because God Lives in Us

21 Special Because We Are
     Christ's Body

18 Special Because We Are Adopted

Where We Are Going

In this session we will see that Jesus came to invite us into God's family, and that we need only to believe in Him and receive Him to make it happen.

What We Will Need

- Two 8½″ by 11″ pieces of paper for each
- Crayons or colored pencils
- Pens or pencils for each

In early 1965 there were five of us in the Working family—Dad (Ken), Mom (Miji), Randy (six), Russell (five), and Jeffrey (three). We had no idea when we played on the Northern California beaches that the water from the waves we chased lapped against a finger of land 6,000 miles away. And we had no idea that in the land called Korea there was a boy already living, eating, sleeping, and playing who was to be part of our family. It is hard for us now to imagine those years he spent as Back Keun (Bock Koon) Lee before he got his new name and new life as Jay Kenneth Working.

119

He was only five and a half years old when he came to us, so he doesn't remember much about it, except that he was excited to think he was to be adopted after living in six other situations.

FAMILY SHARING

1. What do you think Back Keun felt when he was told that he was going to be adopted by a family across the sea? (*Note:* If you have small children taking part, explain the word *adopted.* If they know of families with adopted children, mention them.)

2. What do you think the three Working boys felt when they first met their new brother? Do you think everything was fun and easy for the four boys at first?

3. Draw a picture of Back Keun with his new family their first week together. Show things you think would be helpful in welcoming and receiving him. (Have someone read on while the others draw.)

During that same year our family met Someone else for the first time . . . . Oh, we had heard about Him (even celebrated His birthday), but He seemed much farther away to us than Korea before that year. Listen to this description of Him from John's Gospel:

In the beginning was the Word, and the Word was with God and the Word was God. He was in the beginning with God; all things were made through him, and without him was not anything made that was made. In him was life, and the life was the light of men. The light shines in the darkness, and the darkness has not overcome it . . . .

The true light that enlightens every man was coming into the world. He was in the world . . . yet the world knew him not. He came to his own home, and his own people received him not. But to all who received him, who believed in his name, he gave power to become children of God; who were born, not of blood nor of the will of the flesh nor of the will of man, but of God.

And the Word became flesh and dwelt among us, full of grace and truth; we have beheld his glory, glory as of the only Son from the Father. (John bore witness to him, and cried, "This was he of whom I said, 'He who comes after me ranks before me, for he was before me.'") And from his fulness have we all received, grace upon grace. For the law was given through Moses; grace and truth came through Jesus Christ. No one has ever seen God; the only Son, who is in the bosom of the Father, he has made him known.

John 1:1–5, 9–18 RSV

Sometimes we Workings think of the similarities of these two lives that crossed and became part of our own.

4. Fill in the missing words:

> Before we knew him, Jay lived in _____. Jesus lived with
> _____. Jay was called _____ in his other life. Jesus was
> introduced as the _____ in the first sentence of this Scrip-
> ture passage. Jay came to become part of our family—our child. Jesus
> came to give us the power to become _____. This is
> done by receiving and _____ in His name.

Show the picture you made of Jay and his new family. Tell what the family is doing to welcome and receive this new member. What do the words *welcome* and *receive* mean? When each has shared, read again the first two paragraphs of the passage from John and discuss.

5. What have we done in our family to make Jesus welcome? What else could we do?

W E L C O M E   J E S U S

THINGS WE CAN DO:

1. Say *thank You* before meals.

2.

3.

4.

5.

6.

PUT AN ASTERISK (*) NEXT TO THE ONES YOU ALREADY DO.

Together Before God

Now take a paper and write a letter (young children can dictate theirs to someone) to Jesus welcoming Him to His earth, and (if you feel like it) to your home and life. Use your own way of talking. When each has read his letter, join hands and with closed eyes thank Jesus for coming to earth as a man.

Note: Be sure to save all of your letters. You may want to put these up somewhere on display with the pictures you drew, and then save them for your scrapbooks.

■■

19 Special Because We Are Freed From Guilt

■■

Where We Are Going

Guilt is real! All of us have experienced it. So is sin. In this session we consider how to help free others and ourselves from guilt and sin.

What We Will Need

- A timer or clock

Once when I was very young, I heard a boy tell a joke that used a word that my parents had forbidden me to say. One of the other girls in my class wanted to know the joke and begged me to tell her. I really didn't want to say "that word," and I didn't like her very well anyway. But she persisted in turning around and whispering during class, so I finally gave in and told her the joke.

Just then, the teacher looked up and saw us. "What is so interesting that it can't wait until after class, girls?" she asked.

You can imagine my panic as the other girl said, "Miji just told me a joke."

"Well, go on," replied the teacher. "Tell us all so we can laugh, too."

"All right," said my "friend" and told them the joke—bad word and all.

My teacher looked at me with great shock and disapproval. "Miji, I am certainly surprised! And I thought you were such a nice girl."

I remember blushing, and wishing that I could turn into an ant and crawl between the pages of my book. I wanted to be far away from that teacher and the other children in the room. I felt like nothing in my life would ever be the same again.

For weeks after that, I felt sick every morning before school. I wondered if the other teachers and the principal knew. And whether the principal or my teacher would tell my mother. If ever there was a person carrying a heavy load of guilt, it was I.

We moved from that neighborhood shortly after school recessed for the summer, and I remember being very grateful that I wouldn't have to see any of those people again—and that my mother apparently never learned of my awful sin. The pain and humiliation slowly faded as I made new friends, but even years after that the memory of it would dart out at me from some dark corner of my being and cover me with a wave of guilt.

Take a minute of silence, with your eyes closed to think of something you did that caused you to feel guilty. You don't have to share it with anyone unless you want to, but try to remember something specific. (If anyone does want to share his or her memory, make sure that everyone listens with love. Don't express shock or disapproval if you want to keep this important channel of communication open.)

There are two important things about sin and guilt that I learned later that would have helped me if I had understood them then. (*See* Romans 3:23, 24 LB.)

1. *"Yes, all have sinned; all fall short of God's glorious ideal."* I wasn't alone in doing things that made me feel guilty. Everybody in the world has sinned.
2. *"Yet now God declares us 'not guilty' of offending him if we trust in Jesus Christ, who in his kindness freely takes away our sins."* Jesus could take care of my sins!

FAMILY FUN—ROLE PLAYING

CAST OF CHARACTERS	PLAYED BY
Goodie Two-Shoes	_____
Guilty Gus or Gussie	_____
Understanding Sam	_____

Have three members act out this scene: *Guilty Gus* (or *Gussie*) has been caught stealing a candy bar out of *Goodie Two-Shoes*'s desk. *Gus* is very ashamed and sorry about what he did.

Goodie is very critical and wants everyone to know that she (or he) would *never, never, never* do such a thing! (Or *anything* wrong, for that matter.)

Understanding Sam knows how *Gus* feels because he was once caught stealing. He knows that *Gus* is guilty, but he also knows that he himself could have and has done similar things.

Assign the roles giving *Goodie*'s part to the most outgoing one. Take a couple of minutes to "get into character" and then make up what you think each would say and do in a little play for your family. It really doesn't matter if anyone is left in the audience. The play's the thing!

When you are ready to begin, set the timer for five minutes, or appoint someone to call "time." Make sure you reward your actors with a round of applause when they are finished.

FAMILY SHARING

Now see what you have learned from this play.

ASK GUS (or GUSSIE):

1. How he or she felt when Goodie talked about his crime.
2. How he felt about Sam's part in the experience.

ASK ALL:

1. How they like to be treated by others when they have done something wrong.
2. Does this mean that people shouldn't be punished or have a consequence when they do wrong?
3. How does it set you free to know that others do wrong things, too?

The things we have talked about so far have had to do with helping us know how to treat *someone else* when he or she has sinned. What about when *I* sin? "God forgives sins," Pastor Richard Halverson of Washington, D. C., wisely said, "not excuses." Jesus shows us the attitude that we need to have about ourselves in prayer if we truly want to be forgiven:

> Then he told this story to some who boasted of their virtue and scorned everyone else:
>
> "Two men went to the Temple to pray. One was a proud, self-righteous Pharisee, and the other a cheating tax collector. The proud Pharisee 'prayed' this prayer: 'Thank God, I am not a sinner like everyone else, especially like that tax collector over there! For I never cheat, I don't commit adultery, I go without food twice a week, and I give to God a tenth of everything I earn.'
>
> "But the corrupt tax collector stood at a distance and dared not even lift his eyes to heaven as he prayed, but beat upon his chest in sorrow, exclaiming, 'God, be merciful to me, a sinner.' I tell you, this sinner, not the Pharisee, returned home forgiven! For the proud shall be humbled, but the humble shall be honored."
>
> Luke 18:9–14 LB

Together Before God

One way of humbling ourselves before God is to kneel as we talk to Him. (Even the Lord Jesus did this. For instance: See Luke 22:41 as He prepares to go to the cross for *our* sins.) Kneel, and then, with eyes closed, let the leader suggest these steps in prayer, which all will follow either silently or aloud:

1. Present yourself to the Father, telling Him that you, too, are a sinner who falls short of what He wants you to do and be. (Pause until all have an opportunity to pray.)
2. Tell Him about the specific things for which you feel guilty and want forgiveness. (Pause.)
3. Thank Him that He let His only Son, Jesus, come to take our sins on the cross (including the ones you thought about earlier).
4. Thank Jesus that He did this willingly. (Pause.)
5. Now thank Him that you are declared "not guilty" because of your trust in Jesus Christ. (Pause.) *Amen.*

20 Special Because God Lives in Us

Where We Are Going

We want to see that some things are unseen but very real. The Holy Spirit is like that, and is an unseen power in the believer's life. We will discover some of the things that He does in us.

What We Will Need

- Measuring cup and teaspoon
- Tissue paper and scissors
- Soda bottle and cork
- Vinegar
- Sodium bicarbonate (baking soda)
- Water
- Paper and pencil for each

FAMILY FUN

Can something be real and have power if we can't see it? Let's try this simple experiment—*outside,* please, so that you don't knock any plaster off the ceiling!

1. Mix ½ cup vinegar and ½ cup water and pour into the soda bottle.
2. Cut a four-inch square of tissue and put one teaspoon of baking soda on it. Roll the tissue into a tube and twist the ends closed. *Go outside before you proceed.*
3. Drop the soda tube into the bottle and put the cork into the mouth of the bottle.
4. Wait and watch.

You will notice that when the liquid, which is an acid, soaks the paper, it reacts with the base, sodium bicarbonate (baking soda). A chemical reaction begins, which we can see because of the bubbles that form. A gas called carbon dioxide results and pressure builds until the cork "blasts off." We can't see the gas, but the results prove that it is there.

FAMILY SHARING

Can you think of other things that are real but can't be seen or touched? Name some of them: (How about happiness and pain, for starters?)

Were sound waves and television impulses on your list? These are things that require special receiving equipment in order to know that they are there. Radios and televisions are designed to receive these impulses and *we* need the special equipment of eyes and ears to pick them up.

God has given us a supernatural power in the Person of the Holy Spirit. He, too, has a power that we cannot see or touch, but His presence is known because of the results in lives.

And, like the other invisible powers we mentioned, we must have special equipment to receive Him. Read Jesus' words and see if you can tell what that equipment is:

> If you love me, obey me; and I will ask the Father and he will give you another Comforter, and he will never leave you. He is the Holy Spirit, the Spirit who leads into all truth. The world at large cannot receive him, for it isn't looking for him and doesn't recognize him. But you do, for he lives with you now and some day shall be in you.

John 14:15–17 LB

QUIZ: *Give everyone pencil and paper.* Younger children can whisper their answers to an adult to write down—no helping each other.

1. What would you say is the special equipment Jesus says that we have to have before He will ask the Father to send the Holy Spirit? (If needed, read the first verse over again.)

2. Why can't the world receive Him?
3. Why did Jesus say His friends would recognize the Holy Spirit when He came?
4. How long will the Holy Spirit be with a believer, according to this?

Now, these were very hard questions. How many of you were able to answer *one* of them? (Give a round of applause, accompanied by *hoorays* for all who answered one question.) How many tried two? (Applaud.) Three? Four? (A *standing ovation* for anyone answering all of them.) Go around the family and share your answers, seeing if you agreed. Be sure to thank each one for trying and sharing.

When Jay joined our family, we were just new Christians and trying very hard to learn how to obey Jesus by reading His Word. Ken or I would read from the Bible and then ask the boys questions. This was all very confusing to Jay who had never studied about God, and to Jeffrey who was very small (four years old). Randy and Russell, on the other hand, seemed to "hear" things from the Bible that the other two missed over and over again. We thought at the time that it was because they were older than Jeffrey and because Jay was using a new language, English, instead of his original one, Korean.

Then something mysterious happened. Jeff woke us in the middle of the night to tell us that he was worried because he was "trying to love God, but couldn't." He was so upset that we had a special meeting of the family the next day. Russell suggested that Jeff invite Jesus to live in his heart and that Jesus would help him to love God. And Randy said that if he became afraid again, the rest of us could remind him that God now lived in him. He did this and right away the fear was gone.

But the mysterious thing was that, from that day on, Jeff began to understand the things we talked about from the Bible, just as Randy and Russ did.

The next year, without saying anything about it to us ahead of time, Jay walked out onto the field at Anaheim Stadium during the Billy Graham Crusade to say for the first time that Jesus was his personal Saviour, too. And just as suddenly and mysteriously, he began to understand and take part in our family Bible discussions. The missing ingredient hadn't been language or years. It was the decision to love and obey Jesus! To let Him into their lives!

The power of God's Holy Spirit set free in our lives does many things for us. Read these verses and under them write what each says the Spirit does:

[Jesus says:] "But I will send you the Comforter—the Holy Spirit, the source of all truth. He will come to you from the Father and will tell you all about me."

John 15:26 LB

The Holy Spirit tells us about_____.

[Jesus says:] ". . . he [the Holy Spirit] will teach you much, as well as remind you of everything I myself have told you."

John 14:26 LB

The Holy Spirit will_____.

But Christ gave himself to God for our sins as one sacrifice for all time. . . . For by that one offering he made forever perfect in the sight of God all those whom he is making holy.

And the Holy Spirit testifies that this is so, for he has said, "This is the agreement I will make with the people of Israel, though they broke their first agreement: I will write my laws into their minds so that they will always know my will, and I will put my laws in their hearts so that they will want to obey them. . . . I will never again remember their sins and lawless deeds."

Hebrews 10:12–17 LB

Even though God's people were unfaithful, because of Jesus' death on the cross, the Holy Spirit will:

. . . the Holy Spirit helps us with our daily problems and in our praying. For we don't even know what we should pray for, nor how to pray as we should; but the Holy Spirit prays for us with such feeling that it cannot be expressed in words. And the Father who knows all hearts knows, of course, what the Spirit is saying as he pleads for us in harmony with God's own will.

Romans 8:26, 27 LB

The Holy Spirit helps us with our _____ and _____.

The Father understands our prayers because the Holy Spirit:

But we must forever give thanks to God for you, our brothers loved by the Lord, because God chose from the very first to give you salvation, cleansing you by the work of the Holy Spirit and by your trusting in the Truth.

2 Thessalonians 2:13 LB

By the work of the Holy Spirit and by trusting in the Truth, we are:

Now the Lord is the Spirit, and where the Spirit of the Lord is, there is freedom. And we all, with veiled face, beholding the glory of the Lord, are being changed into his likeness from one degree of glory to another; for this comes from the Lord who is the Spirit.

2 Corinthians 3:17, 18 RSV

As we look at Jesus, the Holy Spirit changes us into:

Together Before God

Did you ever realize all that the Holy Spirit does for us?—helping us remember who Jesus is and what He did for us, fixing up our prayers so that the Father hears exactly what we *mean* and not just what we *say*, making us so clean that we can come into God's very presence. . . .

Thank Him now for all the things you've learned about Him—calling Him Counselor or Comforter or Holy Spirit.

██

21 Special Because We Are Christ's Body

██

Where We Are Going

Last time we learned what God the Holy Spirit does *in* us. This time we will see how He works through all of the believers, who are called "the body of Christ," by giving them spiritual gifts to use.

What We Will Need

- Pencil
- Timer or alarm clock
- Piece of gift-wrapping paper or tissue paper for each
- Piece of ribbon or yarn for each
- Separate slips of paper with each one's name written on one
- Hat or large bowl
- Small gift-wrapped "surprise" for each (*see* end of session)

Ken's sister Cora told me recently of some belated presents that she and her husband, Fred, enjoyed. Right after their wedding, they left to spend two years in the marines in North Carolina. They left most of their wedding presents stored in her parents' garage until they came back. What a wonderful time they had getting them out and using them two years later—especially the ones that came after they left, that they hadn't even seen before!

Did you know that *you* might have some presents that you have never opened nor used? Spiritual birthday presents from Jesus! When the Holy Spirit comes to live in a believer on his spiritual birthday, he comes bringing spiritual gifts. Listen:

> Now concerning spiritual gifts, brethren, I do not want you to be uninformed. . . I want you to understand that no one speaking by the Spirit of God ever says "Jesus be cursed!" and no one can say "Jesus is Lord" except by the Holy Spirit.

Now there are varieties of gifts, but the same Spirit; . . . and there are varieties of working, but it is the same God who inspires them all in every one. To each is given the manifestation of the Spirit for the common good.

1 Corinthians 12:1, 3–7 RSV

As each has received a gift, employ it for one another, as good stewards of God's varied grace.

1 Peter 4:10 RSV

However, Christ has given each of us special abilities—whatever he wants us to have out of his rich storehouse of gifts.

The Psalmist tells about this, for he says that when Christ returned triumphantly to heaven after his resurrection and victory over Satan, he gave generous gifts to men.

Ephesians 4:7, 8 LB

The first passage tells us that if we call Jesus our Lord, we *have* the Holy Spirit, and that Spirit brings gifts for us when He comes. Each of us has such a gift and the gifts are different, chosen for us by Jesus Himself. We are to use these gifts for each other to build up Christ's Body here on earth:

Why is it that he gives us these special abilities [gifts] to do certain things best? It is that God's people will be equipped to do better work for him, building up the church, the body of Christ, to a position of strength and maturity; until finally we all believe alike about our salvation and about our Savior, God's Son, and all become full-grown in the Lord—yes, to the point of being filled full with Christ.

Ephesians 4:12, 13 LB

If God's gifts are given *to* people to be used *for* people, let's see what some of them are. Next to each, think of a person you know or have heard of who showed that he or she especially had this particular gift. If you can't think of someone from modern times, consider people in the Bible. You will get points for your answers, so do your best! Share your answers and write them down:

Lists of Spiritual Gifts

GIFT	PERSON(S) USING IT

From Ephesians 4

APOSTLE (one who starts new churches)   _____

PROPHET (one who speaks for God, a
    PREACHER)   _____

EVANGELIST (one who wins people to
    Christ)   _____

PASTOR (caring for God's people as a
    shepherd does sheep)   _____

TEACHER (of spiritual things)   _____

From 1 Corinthians 12

One who gives wise advice   _____
One good at studying and teaching
    spiritual things   _____
One with special faith   _____
One who heals the sick   _____
Miracle workers   _____
One who recognizes good and evil spirits   _____
One who speaks in unknown tongues   _____
One who interprets tongues   _____
One with leadership ability   _____
Administrator (gets others to work)   _____

From Romans 12

One who serves others   _____
One who exhorts (urges along)   _____
One who gives money   _____
One who does acts of mercy   _____
One who gives up life (1 Corinthians 13:3)   _____

Have someone go back and put 5 points next to every place where you
filled in the name of a person from modern times and 3 points next to names
from the Bible. Add 1 bonus point wherever you have two names. Score your
family for understanding of spiritual gifts as follows:

    100–83 points——Superior
     82–70 points——Good
     69–60 points——Fair
     59 or less   ——Try again: go back over your list.

                    Your family score _____

FAMILY FUN

Write the name of each member on separate pieces of paper. Fold them, and
drop them into a hat or bowl. Now give everyone a piece of wrapping paper

and a piece of ribbon or colored yarn. Have each draw a name from the hat. Then, without revealing whose name you have, go find something around the house that you think tells about a spiritual gift possessed by the person whose name you drew. If you truly don't have any idea about his spiritual gifts, give something that tells what gift you would *like* him to have—like a piece of chalk to one who might be a teacher for God someday.

Set the timer for ten minutes. When it rings all must quickly tie up their gifts and come back.

1. Have each person say what spiritual gift he would *like* to have, if able to choose one from the list we studied earlier. Let him tell how he would like to use it. (Read the list over again.)
2. Now exchange the gifts you wrapped for each other and each donor tell why he chose what he did for that person.

Note to parents: Very young children may bring gifts that don't have so much to do with spiritual gifts as with their desire to enter into the fun. Help all to accept the offerings graciously. Even if they don't entirely understand the concept, they will be learning the important art of affirming another family member and expressing their affection in deed and word.

Together Before God

Thank the Lord Jesus that He chose a spiritual gift or gifts for every believer. Ask Him to help you discover yours and to use them to build up His Body here on earth.

Parents: You can help all remember this lesson by giving each a gift-wrapped surprise now. It can be a candy bar, small toy, fruit, or whatever you want.

Unit 6

WE HAVE A FUTURE

22 Not So Far Away

23 Understanding Your Story

24 Treasures Are for Finding

25 God Has a Plan

22 Not So Far Away

Where We Are Going: Planning a Vacation

This is an exercise in working together to set an immediate goal. It will enable everyone to enter into the decision-making process on a subject that is of interest to everyone. Hopefully, each will begin to see that being part of this process doesn't mean having everything "my own way," but rather finding what is especially important to each and working to try to honor this in the final plans.

What We Will Need

- Vacation slides and projector
- Vacation photographs, postcards, or travel magazines
- Special snacks for viewing time (See popcorn-ball recipe at the end of session.)
- Paper and pencil for each—use lined paper which is sectioned off as on page 140

FAMILY FUN

Spend fifteen minutes to a half hour (depending on ages and attention spans of children) looking at slides or photos and postcards from vacations you have taken as a family. If you haven't kept these, look through travel

magazines for scenes that appeal to you. While Dad sets up the projector, the rest of the family might prepare some special snack, such as popcorn balls, candied apples, or another family favorite. If you want to spend more than a half hour looking at slides, finish the rest of this session first and then go back to viewing.

FAMILY SHARING

Now, when you have seen the slides or photos, give each person a paper to fill in as follows:

1.

TEN (OR MORE) THINGS I LIKE TO DO ON VACATION	A	B	C	D
1.				
2.				
3.				
4.				
5.				
6.				
7.				
8.				
9.				
10.				

2. When everyone has written ten or more things on his list, put a mark in columns A through D as follows:
   In A: Put **A** for things you like to do *alone.*
   In B: Put **$** for things that will *cost more than $5.00.*
   In C: Put **H** for things that are *different from what you do at home.*
   In D: Put **R** for things that you find *relaxing or restful.*

3. Now in twos (unless there are only three of you):

• Share what you have written. What do you learn about yourself from the things in the columns?
• Put an asterisk (*) next to your favorite *three* things on the list.

4. Come together as a family now and share the three things each has marked with *. Have someone write these down. Put additional marks next to the ones that are mentioned more than once.

In the days when the Bible was written and when Jesus became a man to visit the earth that He created, few people took vacations as we think of them today. Only the very rich had leisure time. Most people had to work six days a week all year long just to have enough to eat and clothes to wear. Sometimes we forget that this is still true in most parts of the world.

Faithful Jewish families tried to journey to Jerusalem every year for the Passover in the spring as well as for other feasts—the Feast of Dedication in the winter (*see* John 10:22), and Feast of the Tabernacles in the fall (*see* John 7:2–14). Tabernacle means "tent" and each family built a boothlike tent covered with palm branches to live in during the festival. This was sort of like modern backpackers who rely on the materials at hand to set up camp —except that this was in the middle of the city.

All of these "vacations" centered around worship of God. They might be compared to the modern Christian camps. These bring families together for worship, study, and fellowship, and combine this with a location where God's Creation can really be appreciated.

This is another way that families might look at vacation time, as an opportunity to see another part of God's Creation. Read these descriptions of nature by the psalmist:

> Great are the works of the Lord,
>   studied by all who have pleasure in them.
> Full of honor and majesty is his work,
>   and his righteousness endures for ever.
> He has caused his wonderful works to be remembered;
>   the Lord is gracious and merciful."
>
> Psalms 111:2–4 RSV

Read also Psalm 104 from a modern translation like the Living Bible. This Psalm talks about the beauty of all of God's Creation. Sometimes we call "getting away from it all" *recreation* (re-creation). This gives the idea of being refreshed or being renewed during vacation. Think about these elements (worship, appreciation of nature, refreshment, or rest) in the vacations you have taken in the past. (One or more places for each answer. Give everyone a chance to respond.) Write the answers:

1. When did we most enjoy the scenery (God's Creation) on a vacation?

2. Where did we feel the most relaxed and peaceful?

3. When did I enjoy time alone on a vacation? (For a small child this might mean playing alone, supervised from a distance.)

4. When did we have the most fun being together as a family?

Do you begin to see a pattern emerging? Think now about the next vacation you will be taking together.

1. How many days will we have? _____

2. How much time do we want to spend in travel? _____

3. How much money do we have to spend? (*Optional:* according to whether or not you as parents want to include your children in this practical part of the planning.) _____

4. Now, can we think of vacation spots that fit these specifications?

You might also want to take a vacation at home—one in which you stay at home but take local trips and outings during the day.

Together Before God

Pray that God will be with you as you plan a vacation that will help you all feel closer to Him and to each other. Pray that each will be willing to give up some of his desires so that everyone will have a part in the final plan.

Popcorn Balls

1 cup molasses	3 tablespoons butter
1 cup corn syrup	½ teaspoon salt
1 teaspoon cider vinegar	2 quarts freshly popped corn

In a saucepan combine the molasses, syrup, and vinegar. Cook until candy thermometer registers 266°F, or until a small amount dropped into cold water forms a hard ball. Stir in butter and salt, and pour slowly over popped corn, stirring so that each kernel is coated. Butter hands slightly and shape into balls. Cool, wrap balls individually in plastic wrap. Makes 6 balls.

23 Understanding Your Story

Where We Are Going

Last session we experimented with planning a limited but shared goal—we planned for a vacation. This time we will aim at long-range goals by trying to see the previous direction of our lives in such things as important decisions we've made, preferences, and our own abilities. We are making choices all the time that will affect our own future.

What We Will Need

- Plain paper (2 sheets for each)
- Pencils or pens
- Crayons or colored pencils

Most people love stories. It is easy for us to get caught up in a story about people in the movies, television, magazines, or a book from the library. In God's family, we love to hear how someone came to believe in Jesus Christ, and what this meant in the way he lived thereafter. What we forget sometimes is that each of us is part of a very special story, one that is different from everyone else's. The decisions we make—the things we put in our lives—make each story turn out this way or that way. That special story is going on right now, and we can help in the writing of it!

One way that we can begin to understand our own story is to look at what the earlier chapters say. This gives us an idea about what is going to happen next. Let's do that by looking at four memorable turning points in our lives so far—things that changed us or the way life was going.

FAMILY SHARING

Give everyone a blank piece of paper. Fold it in half lengthwise and then crosswise so that you end up with four sections. Number these 1 through 4, and in each do the following:

1. Write about or draw a picture of an important turning point happening in your life. This can be an event or a decision that caused life to

144

be different for you. Then, in each square, show in the picture or answer in writing the following questions:

(a) Where was I and who was involved? The *where* can be either a place, or a state of mind, the way you were feeling.
(b) To what did I say *no* when I chose to go the way I did?
(c) To what did I say *yes?*
(d) How did this affect or change my life thereafter?

Turning-point Examples:

I decided to join in these family times of sharing once a week. (a) I felt that my place in the family wasn't very important, that no one really cared how I felt about anything. (b) I said *no* to watching television one night a week. (c) I said *yes* to trusting my family with what I was thinking and feeling. (d) I know myself and my family better and I want to know more about God. I found that my family does care about what I think, and that others have felt the same way I did.

We moved (a)*from Greenmeadow Lane to Walnut Street* (both the turning point and place). (b) I said *no* to making any new friends because I was afraid I would have to move from them some day (c) I said *yes* to playing alone most of the time. (d) This is making me lonely.

2. Share your written or pictured turning points. Remember (especially parents) that it is not important if you recall the facts of an event one way and someone else another way. This is a time when each is telling how he *feels* about what happened, how it seemed to him. Don't correct each other or tell anyone how he *should have* felt, or how it *really* was.

FAMILY FUN

In a little while we are going to try to write a future chapter of our own stories. But before we go on, let's look at the main character or hero of our stories—ourselves. What do I like? On the back of your paper, answer these questions. Choose one answer in each:

1. I would like to live in a place where the weather is:

   - Sunny and warm most of the time.
   - Crisp and cool.
   - Changing with the seasons, with snow in the winter.
   - Rainy in the winter.

2. If I could live anywhere I wanted, I would live near:

   - The ocean.
   - The mountains.
   - Theaters and museums.
   - Sports centers.
   - The water of an island.
   - Farming country.

3. I would go to a church that:

   - Was quite small and I could know everyone.
   - Was large with lots going on.
   - Where they teach a lot about how to _____.

4. If I wasn't living with this family (assuming that I am grown up), I would live:

   - Alone.
   - With a certain friend (add name) _____.
   - With two or more friends.
   - With someone I don't know yet but who would be _____ ___.

5. I would spend my days (kind of occupation) _____.

6. I would live in this kind of a shelter: _____.

When you have finished, write a short story about yourself, using the things you learned about yourself when you answered the questions. If anyone wants to draw a picture showing what he would like this chapter of life to be like, that is fine. Take about five minutes to describe what you think would be a good life for you as you know yourself now. (It's okay if you change your mind next week or next month or next year as you learn more about yourself.)

Share your stories with each other. Remember not to correct one another. And save these for your scrapbooks!

Over and over again in the Bible we learn that God wants us to choose life. It was never His intention that people should be separated from Him by death or a meaningless life without Him. Jesus says, ". . . I came that they may have life, and have it abundantly" (John 10:10 RSV). We have learned that this quality of life comes from choosing to believe Jesus and obey God. But even before Jesus came to live on earth as a man, God spoke to people through Moses about this:

> See, I have set before you this day life and good, death and evil. If you obey the commandments of the Lord your God which I command you this day, by loving the Lord your God, by walking in his ways, and by keeping his commandments and his statutes and his ordinances, then you shall live and multiply, and the Lord your God will bless you in the land which you are entering. . . . But if your heart turns away, and you will not hear . . . I declare to you this day, that you shall perish. . . . I call heaven and earth to witness against you this day, that I have set before you life and death, blessing and curse; therefore choose life, that you and your descendants may live, loving the Lord your God, obeying his voice, and cleaving to him; for that means life to you and length of days. . . .
>
> Deuteronomy 30:15–20 RSV

"Choose life" also implies that we have the freedom to choose *our* life. Dr. Don Williams, gifted Bible teacher, says that sometimes we forget that *the decision* (to follow Christ) requires *decisions.* That is, a journey is made up of a series of steps taken one at a time, and we choose the direction that they go. We write our own story as we come to turning points—crossroads.

The Apostle Paul says that we not only *have* a story, but that we *are* a story, a letter written to the world, if we are followers of Jesus:

> . . . you are a letter from Christ delivered by us, written not with ink but with the Spirit of the living God, not on tablets of stone but on tablets of human hearts.
>
> 2 Corinthians 3:3 RSV

Together Before God

Now, ask God to help you plan your life, one pleasing to Him. Ask Him to help you with decisions about your work, your friends and even your (future) husband or wife. Thank Him that He has special plans—just for you.

24 Treasures Are for Finding

Where We Are Going

In this session we want to see that in each of our lives and persons are treasures that God wants us to discover and present to Him for polishing.

What We Will Need

- Paper and pencils or pens for each
- Grocery bags
- Timer or alarm clock
- A special prize (one that would be appropriate for anyone in the family, like something to eat, stationery, and so on) and small "good try" prizes for everyone else

We Workings love to go to my cousins' (Tom and Jeaneen Tucker) farm in the Teanaway Valley of the Washington Cascades. Besides the spectacular natural beauty of the area, we love it because we feel like we are on a con-

tinual treasure hunt whenever we leave our house next to the river. Mountain trails lead to roofless log cabins, where in our imagination we see the trappers or settlers who lived there so long ago. Or we come across an abandoned logging camp almost covered over with blackberry vines and think of the bustling activity of the men long gone.

Once in a while, if we are lucky, we find a dented enamel pan or an old olive-oil tin or (best of all) a bottle turning colors from age. These things evoke in us feelings of both a bond with the past and excitement about what we might find next. But in order to experience this sense of being part of the history of this place we had to *discover* the things that were already there, waiting for us to notice them. If we merely drove by in a car, or never got down off our horses, we would see the same mountains and river, but not the things that speak of the lives of the people who were here before us.

Sometimes people go through their own lives "riding in a car" or "high upon a horse," we might say, completely unaware of the treasures around them waiting to be discovered and used. Once we uncover them, we can take them with us into the future.

FAMILY FUN: TREASURE HUNT AT HOME

Let's see if we can discover some of the treasure around us now. And there will be a prize for the one who finishes first. Each person is to take a paper bag and a list of the treasures he is to find. (Either write out the lists ahead of time or dictate them now.) Then send everyone to hunt, setting a timer or alarm clock for 15 minutes. Bring back:

1. Something that you are proud of making yourself or that *reminds* you of something you once made.
2. Something that reminds you of a special family time.
3. Something that reminds you of God's love for you.
4. Something that tells what kind of parent you want to be (now or when you grow up).

The first person back with his treasures wins the special prize and the first chance to share what is in his bag. The others get a "good try" prize after showing their treasures in the order that they returned from the hunt.

FAMILY SHARING

Let's try to see some other treasures in our lives. Finish these sentences and write down your answers on separate pieces of paper for each.

1. My parents are a treasure in my life because _____.
2. My family is a treasure because _____.
3. The good times are a treasure because_____.
4. The mistakes that we make are also treasures because _____.
5. Listen to what the Bible says about having Jesus inside your life:

> For God is at work within you, helping you want to obey him, and then helping you do what he wants.
>
> Philippians 2:13 LB

Now, how would having Jesus in your life be a treasure?

6. There is another very exciting thought that we find in God's Word. Did you know that *you* are a treasure *yourself*, that God has put into the world and into the future? Think of it. When He planned the world He considered what it would be like *without* YOU and what it would be like *with* YOU and He chose to include you.

And like some treasures, we were also buried when we were baptized. "We were buried therefore with him [Jesus] . . . so that as Christ was raised from the dead by the glory of the Father, we too might walk in newness of life" (Romans 6:4 RSV).

The old pans and bottles that we dug up in the mountains of Washington were not treasures before they were buried. They were empty and useless. When we decide to make Jesus' death on the cross and burial count for our sins in life, we also can count on the same Resurrection and new life. "For if we have been united with him in a death like his, we shall certainly be united with him in a resurrection like his" (Romans 6:5 RSV). Our lives that were empty and useless are now treasures.

And just as our old bottles didn't look like much when we took them from the ground, before we polished them, we are in for surprises as we see the changes that will go on in us as we go through life with Jesus:

> Beloved, we are God's children now; [but] it does not yet appear what we shall be, but we know that when he [Jesus] appears we shall be like him. . . .
>
> 1 John 3:2 RSV

How can we help each other and ourselves to change into what God plans for us to be? Take this TRUE/FALSE test together and talk about why you answered the way you did:

1. When we accept someone's apology for something he did wrong, this helps him to change.   TRUE   FALSE
2. Once I say something, I have to stick with it forever.   TRUE   FALSE
3. When someone does something I like, it helps to tell him about it.   TRUE   FALSE
4. When someone does something I don't like, it helps to tell him.   TRUE   FALSE
5. It helps a person to change when I keep telling embarrassing things he did a long time ago.   TRUE   FALSE
6. Name-calling keeps someone from changing when he really wants to.   TRUE   FALSE

Together Before God

Let's close with prayer in which we thank God for a treasure we see in someone else in our family circle. Let's also invite God to uncover the treasures in ourselves and to polish us by showing us what He wants to change about us.

■■

25 God Has a Plan

■■

Where We Are Going

As much as we enjoy life, we can't help but notice that it is sometimes unfair. It is encouraging to read in God's Word that He is aware of this and has a plan. If we know this and believe it, we can be part of it.

What We Will Need

- Pencil
- Activity Box materials (*See* end of session.)

Jeffrey has a condition, epilepsy, that makes him fall suddenly and violently. He has often been hurt in these attacks. The same things that caused this keep him from learning the way other children do. He sees words backwards sometimes, and a word that he learned yesterday looks completely new to him on the page today.

Jay was born in a country where the medicine that keeps American children from catching the crippling disease, polio, was scarce. When he was a baby, he became sick and was left with legs that needed to be supported with braces in order for him to walk. He has spent many painful hours recovering from operations that are helping him to get around better.

Everyone has in his family or among his friends someone who seems to have been cheated in life. *Can you think of someone you know?* More and more we see in the newspapers and magazines pictures of people who live in places where there is not enough food to keep them alive. There are wars and earthquakes and floods that cause tragedy in countless lives.

Is heaven so far away that God can't see these things? Did Jesus forget about the people He came to save? No! The Good News is that He has had a plan all along. Long before the Prophet Amos cried for "justice [to] roll down like waters, and righteousness like an ever-flowing stream" (Amos 5:24 RSV), God planned a kingdom where:

. . . Behold, the dwelling of God is with men. He will dwell with them, and they shall be his people, and God himself will be with them; he will wipe away every tear from their eyes, and death shall be no more, neither shall there be mourning nor crying nor pain any more, for the former things have passed away.

Revelation 21:3, 4 RSV

FAMILY SHARING

1. Name some of the things that you think will *not* be in God's new city:

We have often considered how trusting in Jesus Christ helps us now, but as Paul says, "And if being a Christian is of value to us only now in this life, we are the most miserable of creatures" (1 Corinthians 15:19 LB). And Jesus Himself wanted us to know about His future plans for us:

[Jesus said:] "Let not your heart be troubled. You are trusting God, now trust in me. There are many homes up there where my Father lives, and I am going to prepare them for your coming. When everything is ready, then I will come and get you, so that you can always be with me where I am. If this weren't so, I would tell you plainly. And you know where I am going and how to get there."

"No, we don't," Thomas said. "We haven't any idea where you are going, so how can we know the way?"

Jesus told him, "I am the Way—yes, and the Truth and the Life. No one can get to the Father except by means of me. If you had known who I am, then you would have known who my Father is. From now on you know him—and have seen him!"

John 14:1–7 LB

2. If there weren't a life after this one, do you think Jesus would have told His disciples? Find something in the passage above that shows this:

3. Who is going to take us to this new home where there is no pain or crying?

   If you want to know what kind of bodies we will have there, have someone read aloud 1 Corinthians 15:35–57 from the Living Bible or another
modern translation.

4. Think about this place where there is no danger and you have all the time
   you want to do things. Go around the circle and tell what you would do in
   one such "day" in eternity if you could go anywhere and do anything you
   wanted. Would you fly, for instance, as I have always wanted to do? Who
   would you like to see enjoying his or her new spiritual body in heaven?
   (I, of course, think of my Jeff and Jay.)
5. If you could choose any one person to spend a "day" talking with, who
   would you choose and what one subject would you like to discuss?

Together Before God

When all have shared, hold hands in a circle and thank Jesus for the place
He is fixing for *you* right now. Ask Him to help you to be ready when He
comes for you.

FAMILY SHARING

That brings up the question, how are we to show that we are ready? Listen
to these words of Jesus:

> When the Son of man comes in his glory, and all the angels with him, then
> he will sit on his glorious throne. Before him will be gathered all the na-
> tions, and he will separate them one from another as a shepherd separates
> the sheep from the goats, and he will place the sheep at his right hand, but
> the goats at the left. Then the King will say to those at his right hand,
> "Come, O blessed of my Father, inherit the kingdom prepared for you from
> the foundation of the world; for [*see* FAMILY FUN for how to fill blanks]
>
> I was hungry and you gave me food, _____
>
> I was thirsty and you gave me drink, _____
>
> I was a stranger and you welcomed me, _____
>
> I was naked and you clothed me,_____

I was sick and you visited me, _____

I was in prison and you came to me." _____

Then the righteous will answer him, "Lord, when did we see thee hungry and feed thee, or thirsty and give thee drink? And when did we see thee a stranger and welcome thee, or naked and clothe thee? And when did we see thee sick or in prison and visit thee?" And the King will answer them, "Truly, I say to you, as you did it to one of the least of these my brethren, you did it to me."

Matthew 25:31–41 RSV

FAMILY FUN

Look at the list of things that Christ Jesus says He wants to find us doing when He comes for us. Next to each thing, write something that your family can do in your own neighborhood. Is there a prison-visitation program in your city for which Father could volunteer for one evening? If not, think about shut-ins who are in a different sort of prison.

Have you ever made an Activity Box for a sick child? The Bocks have delighted many children by gathering "junk" for them to assemble in all sorts of artistic and fun ways. Why not put such a box together now and keep it for a time when some child you know is shut in with illness. (Or if you would rather, contact a local hospital and ask if such a gift would be welcome—perhaps for a child without many visitors or one with a long-term hospitalization.)

Activity Box

Felt patches or squares	Old greeting cards, fronts only
String and yarn	Construction paper
Buttons	Paper lace doilies
Fabric with patterns	Colored cellophane
Pieces of lace and ribbon	Pieces of wrapping paper
Cellophane tape	Paints, crayons
Glue or paste	Children's scissors

Or, you name it!

■■

26 Evaluation
What Have We Learned?

■■

Where We Are Going

Education *equals* experience *plus* evaluation, according to Dr. Edward Lindeman, the president of Whitworth College, Spokane, Washington. To learn from something, we must try it and talk about it. This lesson will let us share what we have each learned during these family sessions together.

What We Will Need

- Piece of paper with shield drawing (as on page 158) for each
- Pencils
- Ingredients for special treat (*See* FAMILY FUN.)

FAMILY SHARING

Hand out the shields and pencils. Have each fill his as follows:

1. Draw something that represents your favorite *Happiness Is* . . . time together.
2. Show something new you learned about another family member during these times.
3. Show something representing a new thing you learned about yourself.
4. Draw something that shows how you see your family now.
5. Think up one word that you think describes your family.

Take ten or fifteen minutes for everyone to fill in the sections of the shield. Then go around the circle and share what you have drawn and why you each chose the symbols you did. Don't expect everyone to see things the same way. Differing viewpoints give a richer, broader picture of things. Many things can be different and true at the same time. Then hang these shields as a reminder display for a week. When you take them down, put them in this book for keepsakes.

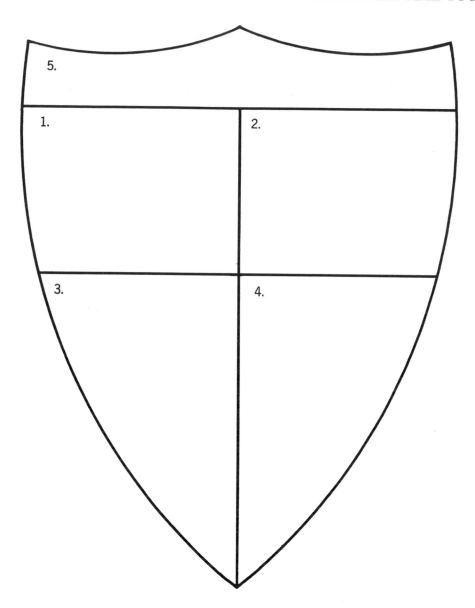

The shield helped us see what we have learned about the family we live in. Now let's think about the larger family, *God's family,* and see what we know. What are the names we have used for God during these sessions? (Think of the three Persons of God.) Write them in the space below:

Now see who can answer these questions. (Ask for volunteers.) Write your answers.

1. In what way are all believers "adopted children"?

2. Why should people be concerned about the earth and what happens to things like forests, rivers and animals?

3. All people have *talents*, but only certain people have spiritual gifts. Why is that?

4. How can people get rid of guilt when they have sinned?

5. How can we show that we belong to Christ Jesus? What sorts of things can we do in the world?

Together Before God

Using one of His names that seems special to you, thank God for the other members of your family, saying what you especially appreciate about each. Do this out loud. Thank Him for drawing you closer to each other and Him.

FAMILY FUN

Since this is the last session of *Happiness Is a Family Time Together*, how about a special treat—do-it-yourself ice-cream sundaes. Put out two or three flavors of ice cream and toppings, bananas, nuts, coconut and. . . . Let each assemble his or her own special concoction. Just like you in your family, each will be a little different, but very, very good!